NatWest Small Business Bookshelf

This series has been written by a team of ⸺
years' experience and are still actively involved in the day⸺
problems of the small business.

If you are running a small business or are thinking of setting up your
own business, you have no time for the general, theoretical and often
inessential detail of many business and management books. You need
practical, readily accessible, easy-to-follow advice which relates to your
own working environment and the problems you encounter. The
books on the NatWest Small Business Bookshelf fulfil these needs.

- They concentrate on specific areas which are particularly problematic
  to the small business.

- They adopt a step-by-step approach to the implementation of sound
  business skills.

- They offer practical advice on how to tackle problems.

The authors

David Royall is a lecturer with experience in teaching business studies and computer programming. He undertakes PC consultancy work for a number of small firms.

Mike Hughes has over 30 years' experience in the computer field, and has taught mathematics and computing for almost 20 years. He is co-director of a software development company and acts as a consultant in computer technology.

Other titles in this series:

A Business Plan
Book-keeping and Accounting
Exporting
Franchising
Hiring and Firing
Purchasing for Profit
Retailing
Selling
Small Business Finance
Small Business Survival
Starting Up
Understanding VAT

NatWest Small Business Bookshelf

Computerisation in Business

David Royall · Mike Hughes

Pitman

Pitman Publishing
128 Long Acre, London WC2E 9AN

A Divison of Longman Group UK Limited

First published in Great Britain in association with the National Westminster Bank,
1990

© Longman Group UK Ltd 1990

A CIP catalogue record for this book is available from the British Library.

ISBN 0-273-03247-X

Typeset, printed and bound in Great Britain

Contents

Preface   vii

Part one: Making a sound start

The decision to computerise   3   1

The technology of microcomputers   9   2

Some business applications   18   3

Getting started with your computer   36   4

Part two: Acquiring and implementing a computer system

Initial costs of computerisation   47   5

Your first steps to computerisation   57   6

A case study   67   7

More on costs of computerising   78   8

Part three: Installing and running a computer system

Practical aspects of installing a computer   95   9

Staff training   103   10

Implementing an applications package   109   11

A further case study   114   12

Part four: The next steps

Looking after your system   123   13

Extending your system   132   14

When things go wrong   137   15

A final case study   142   16

Appendices: 1 A glossary of computing terms;
2 An outline of the Data Protection Act;
3 Sources of information;
4 A brief guide to using MSDOS;
5 Details that might appear on a tender document   149

Index   175

Preface

Developments within the computer industry over recent years have led to computerisation becoming a practical prospect for any business whatever its size.

The computer is the most versatile piece of machinery that man has ever developed. There are thousands of possible applications for which programs can be (and have been) written. The vast majority of these applications are specialised and we could not and would not claim to pass judgement on them. However, the vast majority of modern businesses require computers to help with day-to-day chores such as bookkeeping, word processing, stock control, production control and perhaps manipulating management information. The computer, controlled by special programs, is the pre-eminent tool for all of these jobs.

Although cheap hardware has been available for at least a decade, it is the wide acceptance of the IBM standard which has really brought this about; a standard that has been enhanced by the growth of a large number of cheap 'clones' copying this standard. Its general acceptance has led to the emergence of an enormous range of software for businesses. This includes both general purpose packages relevant to any business and many specialist packages for businesses which operate in a particular field. At the same time, the range of choices available in hardware has also been increasing, with more and more manufacturers building products which conform to the IBM standard.

So, although hardware and software choice is generally good, offering the opportunity to buy products at competitive prices and which relate well to the purchaser's own requirements, it has made the purchase decision even more difficult for many potential users.

This book is not intended to be a 'computer book for business people' but rather a 'business book about computers'. It attempts to present the alternatives available and to guide you, the business man or woman, as you contemplate either the introduction of a computer system into your business for the first time or the improvement of the computing power available in your business.

It is our belief through practice and experience that business people should not have to become computer experts in order to derive significant benefits from the introduction and use of computers. It should merely be necessary for them to understand the potential of the technology and 'know how to drive' it.

As a result, this book concentrates on matters of practice relevant to the non-technical business person. It aims to provide a step-by-step guide from making the decision that computerisation is worth investigating; through deciding what to buy; buying a system; getting it installed and working; to managing the system thereafter. In order to assist you to place much of the material into an understandable context, the book uses a number of case studies and highlights some of the principal obstacles encountered by businesses when introducing computer based systems.

However, it is necessary to explain to some degree the technology itself. Some understanding is required in order to run a system, as well as to be able to read product literature and deal with computer sales people; several more 'technical' chapters in this book will help you with that understanding. Should you have difficulty with any computer jargon (although this should be explained in the text), please refer to Appendix 1 which is a glossary of key computer terms.

David Royall
Mike Hughes
January 1990

PART ONE

Making a sound start

This first part of the book aims to acquaint you with the benefits that a computer might bring to a business and explains how to go about making a start in the process of computerisation.

The technology is discussed in a brief and practical way, emphasising the point that computers are general purpose tools which can perform almost any task which involves manipulating information.

This part discusses the potential uses a computer can be put to in a typical business, drawing on examples from all areas of business operations such as sales, marketing, purchasing, stock control, personnel, general administration and financial control, as well as accounting.

It then considers the basis on which the decision to computerise should be made; that is, how to assess the potential impact on the bottom-line profitability of the business, whether through direct cost reduction or through increased efficiency leading to a more competitive business.

1 The decision to computerise

What's in it for me? □ Does my business need a computer?
□ Action points □ A few words on reporting □ What are the
benefits?

What's in it for me?

Correct implementation and efficient use of a computer within a
business can lead to substantial overall savings in time and money.
They can lead to greater management awareness and can open up
opportunities that would otherwise go unnoticed or be beyond the
capability of the business. There are, however, many pitfalls. The
main theme of this book, therefore, is to help you to decide on
whether you could benefit from computer technology and, if so, how
you should go about acquiring and commissioning a computer
system.

Does my business need a computer?

This can be a difficult question to answer if the responsible people
are not aware of what a computer can do and of its limitations.
As a starting point, it is often a good idea to approach a computer
consultant who will be able to discuss your business needs and give
guidance on how a computer can benefit your business. An
alternative method for you to learn how a computer goes about
performing tasks, and perhaps gain some experience, is by attending
exhibitions or enrolling on a short course at a local college. Also,
it is always useful to contact friendly business associates who use
computers in order to benefit from their experience; if you do not
have such a contact, then a consultant should be able to arrange
such a visit for you. Take note of their successes and try to see where
they were astute in their approach and, if possible, find out where
the blame lies for any faults, defects or teething problems.
As a word of warning, you should never over-rely on a vendor's

or sales person's word that a system offered for sale is adequate for your particular business. Such a supplier should not be your 'first port of call' when seeking help and advice. At a later stage, a vendor's assurance that a system is adequate and can cope with your business needs could form the basis of a contractual clause.

An important activity in the early stages is to assess exactly what the computer system ought to do; in other words, what work the computer can do for the business. Examine where in the business problems are arising; perhaps the business is not coping well with the processing of sales orders or the issue of invoices. Many firms have looked towards computers as a way of getting around mounting problems. But beware. Computers are not of themselves a panacea and problems may have complex roots which a computer will not address.

Establishing the amount of work that has to be done will help vendors ensure that an adequate system is provided, in the same way as a business decides to purchase a motor vehicle only after it has some idea of the amount of work the vehicle will be required to do, the amount of freight it has to carry. A corresponding set of criteria applies to the choice of a computer system.

For example, a firm might decide that computerising the sales ledger or stock system could benefit the firm. It is important to think in straight forward and non-technical terms such as:

● Can the existing manual system do what we want it to do?
● Does the processing of transaction details take up too much time?
● Does the existing system supply all the information that is needed from it and can we improve on this?
● Can the existing system cope with the current work load and, just as important, will it cope with future increases?

Identifying such areas for computerisation and asking such questions of your manual system is a good and sound first step towards deciding whether computerisation can benefit a business. You may well find that the hardest part of this is trying to establish exactly how your business goes about processing information. If the business cannot answer such fundamental questions, then difficulties will be encountered when trying to introduce a computer system to perform the functions for it. Organise your thoughts using the action list below. You may find that, having undertaken this exercise, you will be able to improve the existing manual systems without a computer ever being employed.

Action points

1. If you are serious about employing a computer for use within your business, then it is a good idea to write down the kind of processing activities that your business has to carry out. In other words, make a list of headings to show those areas where information is handled or processed, such as:

   - Maintaining a sales ledger.
   - Sales order processing.
   - VAT returns.
   - Invoicing.
   - Managing a bought ledger.
   - Keeping stock records.
   - Producing a 'mail shot'.
   - Keeping an appointments diary.
   - Payroll.

2. Outline the current processing activities within your business. Apart from being of use later on in the computerisation process, this outline will help you develop a clearer idea of those activities that will have to be converted for handling in a computerised system.
3. List the documents and actual information used within each defined area of activity. This will help to identify the nature of information that a computer might have to handle.
4. Quantify the information that you handle, e.g. how many invoices, how many stock movements. The purpose of this exercise is to identify the size and power of the system that may be required to computerise your business activities.

The essence of this is to encourage you to think about the information processing problem that exists in your business. Only when responsible people within the business itself have a clear idea of the size and nature of its activities can they convey such facts to a vendor and become the beneficiaries of a computer system that works effectively for the business.

A few words on reporting

Throughout this book you will see the word *report* used quite frequently. Our use of this word is probably far more general than yours. In a non-computing context, a report is often a long piece of text structured in sentences and paragraphs giving a description or explanation of an event. In computing, however, a report can be something quite sophisticated such as a summary of all those stock items that appear to be short in supply; alternatively, it can be a simple price list.

What are the benefits?

Buying a computer, switching it on and then trying to use it will not by itself bring a whole host of benefits to a business. They can only come about if a business adopts a sound approach to its acquisition, finance and implementation. The benefits that *can* be derived are many and far reaching. Some of the more obvious ones are now discussed.

Save time on transactions processing

A computerised system simply performs the storage, retrieval and processing of data electronically; this means that the data will be processed much more quickly than if it were done manually. However, transactions and amendment details have somehow to get into the process in the correct form, in the correct order and speedily. For example, a computer can allow you to print invoices easily and quickly provided the computer can quickly retrieve the customer information and stock information. Just as important for a computer system to be successful is the need to ensure that such information is up to date and correct. Although there is scope to use electronic methods to enter some of these details, a good deal of human initiative and an organised way of doing things will be required. Moreover, the necessary equipment does not come cheap.

Speed of response

There is a tremendous potential for saving time, when so little human intervention is required, in printing standard letters to groups of customers, extracting price lists, compiling customer statements and producing management reports such as balance sheets and trading and profit and loss accounts whenever they might be useful. Indeed, effective reporting can make major improvements in the decision making process.

For example, a computer system should be capable of detecting when key stock items are in danger of running out or when a customer appears to be running up excessive debts with the company. Timely reports, which are simple to produce on the computer, offer the chance to take action before things get out of hand.

Better Control

Budgetary control is another area where the computer can be of great benefit. For instance, many business expenses can get out of hand if they are not checked at regular intervals. An activity that the computer is well adapted to performing is known as *exception reporting*; this is the process of issuing early warning signals when something appears to be out of order. In a manual system, many errors or unwanted transactions can go unnoticed until the repercussions are serious or have already incurred unnecessary costs to the firm. There is still the potential for error in a computerised system, but built-in checking systems can bring many of them to the attention of the user.

Accuracy

Improved accuracy may be one of the more obvious benefits of any kind of computer system; this is especially the case with accounting and financial analysis, where numerous calculations have to be carried out.

Bigger volumes handled

For many businesses, the need to produce monthly and annual returns such as VAT and payroll stoppages can be time consuming, tedious and unrewarding. The use of a computer system to assist in this process can effectively speed up the process and reduce the monotony of producing lengthy and uninteresting reports with large amounts of figure work. In many cases, firms find that they can use computer printouts or even data on computer disks instead of completing official forms.

More job satisfaction

More job satisfaction and more effective use of operator time can be added bonuses of computerisation. For example, if a firm computerises its stock records, the job of keeping records properly maintained will be much the same as was the case in the manual system. However, with instant reporting facilities available, so that a list of all stock items in short supply can be quickly produced, the work is much less laborious, thus allowing an operator to keep a much closer check on stock levels. Also, if time can be saved in producing stock reports, the operator may have more time to 'chase up' suppliers who are not delivering on time and 'shop around' the market for better suppliers and products.

Many more benefits of computerisation should become apparent as you read through this book. It is worth noting that the extent and kind of benefit will vary from firm to firm. It may well be the case that some firms will be unable to derive any benefit at all from computers. Throughout the book, we have introduced case histories as a way of gaining a much better appreciation of the possible benefits, as well as the problems, from computerisation of business activities.

You will come to appreciate the fact that benefits of a computer depend heavily upon the way the business organises its information processing activities. As we have already hinted, extracting sophisticated reports quickly will be of no benefit if the information being retrieved is badly out of date or contains major errors. A business must organise itself in such a way that, if information needs to be entered into the computer quickly, then this actually occurs and in such a way as to preserve accuracy. For example, if the success of a stock system is dependent upon stock movements being fed into the computer as and when they occur, then the facility should be made available for this to happen. This, in turn, can only happen if the people involved in setting up the system either have or are given the knowledge about these procedures in the first place.

Once a computer system is working properly, managers will often find themselves extracting information that under a manual system could not be achieved within a useful time frame. The improved reporting and analysis that can be achieved by computerisation should improve the whole decision making process within a firm.

2 The technology of microcomputers

Computer systems ◻ What is computer hardware? ◻ What is computer software? ◻ Simple computer systems ◻ Choosing your system ◻ Printing ◻ Storing information ◻ What is a hard disk? ◻ What is a floppy disk? ◻ Tape streamers ◻ Computer memory ◻ Speed ◻ Mouse ◻ Summary

Computer systems

When one considers a new system (whether computer based or manual), one has to place notional boundaries in order to be aware of what is inside the system and what is outside. Management of a system will only be able to control those things *within* the system. Those outside are beyond the control of the system. A business computer system will consist of a number of primary items or procedures, i.e. the computer hardware, the programs (software), the users who decide what the system is to do from time to time and who supply the hardware and software with data to process, the rules and regulations that the users are required to comply with.

What is computer hardware?

A basic requirement will, of course, be for computer hardware. Hardware consists of the physical components – those bits you can feel and kick. Software is basically intangible; it is a list of instructions which control the activities of the hardware. These lists of instructions are, of course, known as programs. All computer hardware needs programs if it is to be of any value. The versatility of a given piece of computer hardware arises because it can be made to perform an enormous range of activities simply by changing the program it obeys. Simply by placing it under the control of different programs you can make the same piece of hardware play chess with you, do your accounts and print your letters.

Hardware, because of its physical presence, is probably easiest to understand. For example, a keyboard lets you key data into the computer; a screen displays information keyed in and the results of the information which has been processed.

What is computer software?

With software, on the other hand, it is not easy to define the functions of the various categories; in fact, it is not always clear which category a piece of software falls into. In spite of some overlaps, however, software can generally be broken into distinct levels.

The first level is the computer's *operating system*. This software, as its name suggests, will *control* all parts of the computer system and therefore provides an environment in which the user's application programs can function (or operate); such as, keyboard input, screen output, printing and the manipulation of data internal to the computer itself. Each computer system must have some sort of operating system, but they will not all have the same one. There are, indeed, many operating systems, e.g. the MicroSoft Disk Operating System (MSDOS), CDOS from Digital Research, Operating System/2 (OS/2) from IBM and Xenix again from MicroSoft. Such operating systems are designed for different types or groups of hardware and have gradually changed in nature over the years. As computers have become more advanced and their operating environment has changed, the operating system has also had to change.

The second level of software is the *Applications Package*. This works under the control of the operation software by offering the added features required to perform specific tasks, such as accounting and stock control. When purchasing an applications package it is important to ensure that the correct package is purchased to match the operating system. In turn, the operating system must match the computer system. In other words, *compatibility* must exist between the hardware, the operating system and the applications package.

Simple computer systems

When hardware and software are combined, we have an elementary computer system, the only function of which is to process data. Change the process by changing the software and feed the system with the same data and a different program to perform a different task. If the system is under the control of a sales program then it follows a simple process:

- Data, such as details of sales to customers and payments made by customers, is fed into the computer system.
- The machine stores this data.
- It then manipulates (or processes) this data and produces useful documents such as invoices, customer statements and VAT statements.

Choosing your system

Initially, it is best to disregard the operating system and hardware when trying to decide on the type of computer system to acquire. In other words, first determine the applications required and, in turn, the applications packages best suited to the business. Once these decisions have been made, the choice of operating system and the range of suitable hardware are narrowed significantly, thus making the choice much easier. The application, therefore, is the focal point of *any* computer system.

Another factor that will influence the choice of operating system and of hardware is the amount of work a system has to do. The operating system must have the versatility required by the applications package and the hardware must be capable of supporting the software. Also, the computer system will need to have sufficient storage to cope – a good reason for hiring the services of a consultant with a good deal of experience who will have the skills to judge such requirements and make appropriate allowances.

The types of system that would normally meet the needs of most small to medium sized businesses fall into one of three categories: stand alone, network and multi-user or multi-tasking systems.

1. **Stand alone.** Such a system will consist of one screen, one keyboard, one, or preferably two, disk drives and enough memory to run the software and hold the data required. For a firm with relatively small data processing requirements and no need for more than one operator to be at the keyboard at any time such a system could prove adequate.

   Generally speaking, such systems are adequate only for rather small firms employing only a handful of clerical staff.

However, a large firm may opt for a number of stand alone systems working in isolation rather than a network of linked systems, described below.

2. *A network of micros*. This allows the linking of microcomputers in such a way that they are able to share information and centralise the distribution of data and program control. In other words, someone working at a computer on a network system that supports an accounts application can update information on (say) a customer and allow any other person at a different machine to be aware of the update on inspecting that customer account. Such a set-up is of particular use in a firm that requires an application to be used by more than one person simultaneously or that requires the application to be divided between a number of staff. It also allows management the facility of extracting reports without having to disturb other staff.

   The number of microcomputers on such networks is not limited, and can be altered to suit the requirements of the firm. Small networks may have from two to ten machines linked together. Firms should always take advice when deciding on the number of microcomputers to network together; too many on a network can, at times, lead to congestion and serious reductions in processing speed. Building up a network of computers can be a complex job requiring sound advice.

3. *Multi-user, multi-tasking*. Such a set-up appears to be much the same as a network. The difference lies in the fact that the system is one computer with a number of *terminals* attached to it. In other words, each keyboard is not a computer in its own right. Such a system means that the familiar MSDOS operating system normally associated with a microcomputer will be replaced with a different operating system such as Xenix, OS/2 or CDOS. (These operating systems can also be used in networking environments.)

   The main benefit it has over the network is that it is more likely to be a system where you can go to your terminal, flick a switch and be ready to go.

Choosing which type of system is appropriate for a business is not an easy task. It is important to bear in mind that a software package will not work on just any machine. Compatibility across a system is a key issue in the decision making process.

Printing

All business users of computers will need to print information such as customer statements, invoices, order forms, reports. It is worth noting at this point that it is unlikely that computerising the accounting functions will reduce the amount of paper significantly. In fact many new users have found that the computer results in more paper not less.

Different types of printers are available for computer systems. Any firm using computers will need to assess how many printers are required and the quality of printing that needs to be achieved.

The most commonly used printer is the *dot matrix*. Such a printer produces images on paper by means of patterns of dots. Most matrix printers are capable of printing a full page (A4 size) of text in under a minute and of quite acceptable quality. For most accounting function printing output, this kind of printing is both economic and adequate. Stationery for such printers includes continuous paper, which is cheap.

For improved output quality, a *laser printer* is an option. The quality of print is very much better and the machines are not as noisy. They do not use continuous paper, but do accept single sheets of paper of varying sizes, including envelopes. For most business uses this is probably a little extravagant. For graphics output and good quality letter production, a laser printer may be a viable option.

Other types of printers are available for serving differing types of needs. Impact printers that produce typewriter-like print of very high quality are available, but are becoming obsolescent because of competition from lasers. Their main drawback is the noise and vibration that they produce. Ink-jet printers that project minute dots of ink directly onto paper can compete very effectively with lasers where speed is not a prime consideration.

The term *hard copy* is often used to refer to printed output, as opposed to *soft copy* which refers to screen output.

Storing information

One of the main features of a computer is its ability to store data more or less permanently. Magnetic media such as tapes and disks have dominated this field for at least thirty years.

For serious business computing, you will need a hard disk on your stand alone computer and one is mandatory on a file server, which is used to store data for a network of microcomputers. Its purpose is simple — to store the following data:

1. Most of the computer's operating system; some of it is stored internally within the computer.
2. The applications software. Nearly all applications software needs to be stored on the hard disk and called into memory when needed. A hard disk can be read quickly by a computer's processor (in comparison with floppy disks) and will achieve rapid results.
3. Your business data such as your stock records, accounts data and word processed documents. Because this category of data is generated by your business, do not rely too heavily on your hard disk for holding data as it will need to be backed up, otherwise it will be the only copy, leaving your business vulnerable to loss of information.

What is a hard disk?

Hard discs come in different sizes and tend to be measured by their storage capacity, i.e. in megabytes. A megabyte is a measure of how much can be stored on a disk; each megabyte represents just over 1 million individual characters or numbers. Therefore, you can probably gather that a machine marketed as a '30 Mbyte hard disk system' indicates that the computer has a hard disk that holds 30 megabytes (or 30 million characters) of data. To put this in perspective, a page of A4 text might hold about 600 words averaging 6 characters each giving approximately 3,600 (600 × 6) characters; consequently a 30 Mbyte hard disk could hold over 8,300 such pages of text.

The size of disk you need will depend upon the size of business system you wish to run, a decision to be discussed later in this book.

What is a floppy disk?

Floppy disks are much the same as hard disks with the exception that they can be removed from the computer and stored for safekeeping. Their principal uses will be to:

1. Store your disk operating system in case it gets corrupted on the

hard disk. You can restore it from floppy disks.
2. **Transfer applications software on to your hard disk.** When you purchase new items of software, they tend to be dispatched on distribution disks in the form of floppies. After you have *installed* the software on to your hard disk, you can put the floppy disks in a safe place in case any of the software on the hard disks gets corrupted (destroyed or lost).
3. **Back up your business data.** When you are running your computer system, this data will be continually updated. It is important, therefore, that such data is regularly backed up on to floppy disk in case anything should go wrong with it on your hard disk.

Most business machines come equipped with both a hard disk drive with a hard disk fixed into it (sizes vary) and one or two floppy disk drives which can hold removable floppy disks.

Floppy disks required for computer disk drives are made in different sizes, typically 3.5 or 5.25 inches. The amount of storage capacity on a floppy disk will depend upon the type of machine you have, but floppy disks generally hold much less information than hard disks. Their storage capacities typically range from 360 kilobytes (about 360,000 characters) to 1.44 Mbytes.

Tape streamers

Another device for storing information from a computer is a tape streamer. These hold computer data on a tape in much the same way that music is held on a cassette tape. Tape streamers can work at very high speeds and are generally used for backing up large quantities of data from hard disks. Tape streamers cost more than floppy disks but have a higher degree of reliability.

Computer memory

In much the same way that hard disk storage capacity is measured in megabytes, so computer (internal) memory is measured in kilobytes. A kilobyte contains 1,024 characters of data. There are 1,000 kilobytes in one megabyte. Typical values for computer memories range from several hundred kilobytes to tens of megabytes, 640 kbytes being a common amount.

One of the main developments in computer technology has been the very rapid growth of memory size of the machines and the subsequent development of software to take advantage of the facilities that this allows. Such internal memory falls into two categories:

---

1. ROM (read only memory) which will contain programs and data that the machine needs in order to start working. This is part of the computer's operating system, the rest being on the hard disk. As it is *read only memory*, the computer holds this software permanently and it is not possible to alter it without changing the ROM. Your computer will not work without it.
2. RAM (random access memory) starts off empty, when the machine is switched on. It is used to hold:

   (a) The rest of the operating system which is *read* (or loaded in) from a disk. The process of *building* up the operating system in this way is called *booting up* (derived from the old saying about lifting oneself up by one's bootstraps).
   (b) Applications software which is normally read in from the hard disk.
   (c) Business data entered from the keyboard or from other sources. Such data will be directly related to the business and is normally *written* to (or stored on) your hard disk where it has a more permanent home.

Most RAM loses all the data that was stored in it whenever the electrical power is removed. Switching off destroys the data stored in such RAM. It is said to be *volatile*, i.e. it 'evaporates'. Another name is *dynamic RAM*. There is another type called *static* or *non-volatile RAM*, but it is normally used in small amounts for special applications.

A machine advertised as 640K RAM, 32K ROM indicates that the computer has the capacity of 640 kilobytes of RAM available to hold data and has 32 kilobytes of ROM to hold the programs built into the computer. To a business, the details are not really important. All that really matters is whether there is enough RAM to enable you to run the applications efficiently for the business.

Speed

Some attention is often given to the speed of a computer's processor – called its *clock speed*. This is measured in megahertz and gives an idea of the number of elementary operations that the machine can carry out every second. There will be a noticeable difference between a machine working at 8 MHz and one working at 25 MHz. However, for the purposes of most business applications, a more important criterion is the speed at which data can be read from a disk (*disk access*) since such operations are typically more than 10,000 times slower and measured in milliseconds (ms).

Manufacturers are continually increasing disk capacity and providing larger memories for their machines. Technology is also improving both clock speeds and disk access times.

In some of the literature you read, you will see reference made to *bench tests*. These are attempts made by professionals and enthusiasts to compare speeds between computers of different makes. Manufacturers will choose tests that favour their machines and they can also tune their machines to perform exceptionally well if they wish. It is unwise to pay too much attention to such technical details. Reliability of equipment is far more important for business purposes.

Mouse

Many business machines are supplied with a mouse device that can be used with some packages. For most business applications they are unnecessary, but you will need one if you wish to use a graphics package or desk top publishing. Coupled with the use of the keyboard, you will find that a mouse can help you to work very effectively with such packages.

Summary

Computers have developed out of all recognition since the 1960s, the microcomputer, which first appeared in the early 1970s, being the major development. With the development has come a whole new science, and a jargon which has put off many potential users. This chapter has been written simply to give you some understanding of what the jargon is all about. It should be remembered that the computer is very much a tool of the trade and should be approached as such. From the business point of view, it is far more important to become acquainted with what the computer has to offer in the way of faster, more accurate and less demanding processing than how it does what it does.

3 Some business applications

Software and how to choose what you need □ Word processing □ Desk top publishing (DTP) □ Spreadsheets □ Accounts □ Stock control □ Payroll □ Databases □ Bill of materials □ Job costing □ Communications □ Graphics and design □ Some software accessories □ Integrated software □ Standardising software □ Sampling software □ What do you get in a software package? □ The problem of obsolescence □ Summary

Software and how to choose what you need

In the earlier chapters emphasis was placed on deciding what you want to use a computer for. This can be difficult, as you may well now appreciate, if you are not clear what applications have been developed for computers and what they can achieve. This chapter will examine some of the main applications that have typically dominated the business computing market. In effect, there are very few areas of the business market that have not received the attention of software developers.

With each application, there are numerous products available and wide variations among the products. As computers have developed over time with ever increasing memory capabilities and larger mass storage, so the applications for them have taken advantage of the developments and have themselves become bigger and more powerful.

One of the improvements that features strongly in most modern applications is the amount of help available within the packages, many of which allow you to display help screens without having to abandon your work. Such help can be invaluable in the early days of working with a new package. In addition, many packages come with a 'tutor' that is designed to help you to learn how to operate the package as you work with it on the computer.

When purchasing application packages it is important to make sure that what you purchase:

- Does the job you want from it.
- Will serve its purpose for a reasonable amount of time
- Is compatible with your system. For example, if you want to operate the software on a network, then you will need to be certain that your software is a network version.

We will now examine some of the business applications available.

Word processing

Word processing is a relatively straightforward computer application in that it can do what most of us need to do in business: write letters, documents, reports, etc.

A word processing (often abbreviated to WP) package replaces typewriters as a way of producing printed documents. Such an application has a large number of advantages over typewriters. An obvious advantage lies in the ability to read through text easily and alter any mistakes and make changes without having to retype the whole script. Other benefits arise from capability to store work for future reference or to alter it for a different occasion. Such benefits are particularly well illustrated when documents become very long; for shorter documents and memos, you might find that your typewriter is just as effective.

Word processing is a good starting point for anyone new to computing because it is relatively easy to tackle and helps new users familiarise themselves with their computers.

Word processing packages offer an enormous range of capabilities that take a long time to learn fully, if ever. It is uncommon for users of word processing to take advantage of all the facilities available in their package. However, most packages should have the following features in addition to text editing. Some of them may be of value to you and should be considered when purchasing a package:

- Help screens to show you how to perform certain functions available within your package.
- A spelling checker – ideal for someone who cannot spell. It works by scanning your text and comparing it with a dictionary built into your system; usually a file on your disk. If a word cannot be found, then you will be prompted either to replace the word with a correct spelling, to add it to your dictionary or to ignore it. In time you can build a dictionary to suit your business needs.

- A thesaurus to help you to use other words to express yourself better, or even to help solve crossword puzzles.
- A word count to count the number of words in your document.
- Text previews to show you exactly what your text will look like when it is printed on paper.
- Mailing list facilities. Often a situation arises where you want to send a similar letter to a large number of clients, with the only variations being their names and addresses. This allows you to print a standard letter to send to a number of addressees. This takes a little time to master and requires the list of names and addresses to be set up. However, once set up, it can be extremely useful and time saving.

Some well established packages are now available on the market with such names as: Wordstar, Word Perfect, Displaywrite and Wordcraft.

Word processing has introduced a new collection of jargon which should not intimidate new users and can largely be ignored if you simply want to use your word processor to help prepare, print and save documents.

Desk top publishing (DTP)

Desk top publishing can be regarded as being largely an extension of word processing. The differences lie in the way in which it can manipulate text, incorporate graphics and print. Pictures can be scanned by a special device or designs can be developed in a graphics package. They can then be placed in a document and the text made to flow around the pictures, maintaining columnar form in the same way as in newspapers and magazines.

Desk top publishing has developed to take advantage of the improved capabilities of computer hardware and the commercial demands of users for greater flexibility of printed matter from microcomputers.

To use DTP fully, you will need the facilities of a graphics style screen and a laser printer. The reason for this is that DTP allows text to be displayed in many different shapes and sizes (fonts) on the screen at the same time in a similar way as in a magazine or poster.

Matrix printers are not really capable of printing the high resolution often required by DTP users. It is normally necessary to use laser or ink-jet printers with special fonts and special software.

Any business requiring high quality publications can benefit from DTP. It should be remembered, however, that such an application will involve a great deal more effort to acquire the skills to use it.

Over the last few years some packages have become well established in the market such as: Ventura Publisher, Pagemaker, Fleet Street Editor, Gem Desktop and Timeworks.

Spreadsheets

A spreadsheet is the electronic equivalent of an accountant's ledger – a large piece of paper divided by vertical columns and horizontal rows into a grid of cells. The name derives from the spreading of the business's accounts on a sheet of paper. A user can directly enter numbers, formulae or text into the cells. Each cell is referred to by its coordinates, like a map reference or point on a graph. Each cell can contain text, numbers or the results of calculations defined by formulae.

The spreadsheet effectively becomes a screen based calculator which can be printed or, in some cases, displayed as a graph. Any number in the spreadsheet can be changed at any time and the new results will be automatically shown. It allows you to develop 'What if' analyses. 'What if' analysis describes activities such as performing all the calculations necessary to evaluate the proposition 'what if sales were to increase by 10 per cent'. It is the facility of being able quickly to recalculate values according to embedded formulae that makes the spreadsheet a powerful, useful and popular analytical tool. Some spreadsheets are used in order to seek goals. For example, spreadsheets can be set up to depict the sales and costs of a business. A model can be set up to determine what price will maximise profits.

A spreadsheet can be used to hold records such as details of costs accumulated for a specific job. Such information can be altered quickly and can be used as the basis of a contract tender or for the determination of prices.

In practice, spreadsheets will be used for a combination of the above. Spreadsheets are flexible modelling tools which can be readily adapted for many jobs involving repeated numerical calculations.

They are not suitable for highly complex applications and slow down quite markedly when they become large in size.

Some examples of use are:

- Financial plans and budgets can be represented as a table, with columns for time periods (e.g. months) and rows for different elements of the plan (e.g. costs and revenue)

- Tax, investment and loan calculations.
- Statistics such as averages, standard deviations, time series and regression analysis. Statistical functions are built into many spreadsheet packages.
- Consolidation – merging branch or departmental accounts to form group (consolidated) accounts. This involves merging two or more spreadsheets.
- Currency conversion – useful for an organisation with overseas interests.
- Timetabling and roster planning of staff within organisations or departments.

Some well known spreadsheet packages are: Lotus 1-2-3, Supercalc, Multiplan, VP Planner, Quattro, Excell and Sage Planner.

Accounts

Another application area that has been well developed is computerised accounting. The computer, in its role as a very fast calculating machine, is ideally suited to this work. Accordingly, a very wide range of packages is available on the market, and there is one to suit each different type and size of firm. Such packages include Pegasus, Sage, Multisoft and MAP. Accounts packages will normally offer sales, purchase and nominal ledgers either as individual modules or completely integrated. Other modules that are often integrated with the accounting function are payroll, order processing, invoicing, fixed asset register, stock control, bills of materials, etc.

---

1. *Sales*. The purpose of a sales ledger is to record and help manage sales to customers or clients. In their computerised form sales ledgers can normally be used just as effectively for services rendered as they can for goods sold (or they can combine both). They allow a user to create, delete and amend customer details on the ledger as well as to record all transactions between the firm and all its customers. A requirement of the sales ledger is good reporting to ensure the firm can determine, at any time, how much is owed to it and by whom, i.e. it must readily produce a list of debtors. Another facility, vital to almost all firms, is the production of a report to show the VAT collected from its sales. Besides providing for the firm's needs it should also prepare special

reports for those customers and clients to whom the firm is selling. These reports could include details on invoices sent to them in the past and regular statements of account.

If your business requires sales invoicing as well, then you should check whether your package has this facility built in or whether you will require an additional module. Together with sales invoicing, there will normally be a requirement for the system to handle stock recording. This is to allow the invoicing procedures to collect stock and price information from the stock files which will be maintained by the stock recording system.

2. *Purchasing*. The purpose of a purchase ledger is to record and help manage *all* purchases from suppliers. As with sales, a purchase ledger should be capable of being used just as effectively for services acquired as for goods bought, or a combination of both. Such facilities offered by a purchase ledger must allow the user the ability to create, delete and amend suppliers' details on the ledger as well as record all transactions between firm and supplier. An additional requirement would be good reporting on the purchase ledger to ensure the firm is maintaining budgetary control and is not building too much expensive debt. Controlling expenditure will always be an important part of business management, and although an efficient purchase ledger will not, by itself, control expenditure, it should be capable of reporting any problems quickly so they can be rectified. As with the sales ledger, reports on the amount of VAT paid to their suppliers will be vital to most firms.

Businesses may wish to incorporate purchase ordering within the purchase ledger. In some systems it may be incorporated within the purchase ledger or it may entail acquiring an additional module. Also, purchase ordering may well require the maintenance of stock records in order to establish what stock to order and in what quantity.

3. *Nominal ledger*. The nominal ledger is used to record all dealings involving the firm's *assets* such as buildings, stock, work in progress, and its *liabilities*, such as amounts owing to suppliers, loan capital, share capital. In addition, the nominal ledger is used to produce reports such as trial balances, balance sheets, and other information, e.g. telephone or photocopying costs, which might be required from time to time.

The nominal ledger, by its very nature, is very much the pillar of an accounting system where, in varying forms, *all* business transactions will pass. The nominal ledger uses the principle of double entry, a process whereby any transaction

entered to the nominal accounts must have a source and destination (credit and debit). All computerised accounting packages will adhere to the standard double entry procedures and post such things as VAT to the appropriate accounts automatically.

So that it can be used effectively, a computerised nominal ledger should be integrated with sales and purchase so that all sales and purchase ledger transactions can be *posted* automatically to the nominal ledger.

In general, computerised accounts vary quite considerably in their degree of sophistication and the number of functions that are integrated to make up a complete system. Implementing such a system can be done in stages. It is worth noting that some or all of the following functions can be integrated to form a comprehensive accounting and business information system:

- Sales ledger.
- Purchase ledger.
- Nominal ledger.
- Cash book.
- Sales invoicing.
- Sales order processing.
- Purchase order system.
- Stock control.
- Job costing.
- Bill of materials.

It is important, therefore, that when embarking on such computerisation, a business identifies clearly the areas that it needs to integrate and also the amount of activity within each of these areas.

Once an accounting system has been fully implemented, the business should begin to see a marked improvement in its management information systems as well as a fall in auditing costs. The degree of saving and improvement depends on the quality and effectiveness of the system that it has replaced.

Stock control

A stock control system maintains stock records in order to offer control of stock in such a way that:

1. **not too much stock is held, which would place a financial strain on the firm or which might leave it holding obsolete stock;**
2. **does not allow the firm to run out of certain items of stock.**

The aim of controlling stock, therefore, will be to keep stock at its lowest level without impeding either sales or production. This can be achieved only if:

1. **stock records are updated regularly and promptly;**
2. **reporting techniques on stock levels are quick, efficient and timely.**

Recording stock movements promptly is as much a strategic problem as a processing one, which computers alone cannot solve. It may be apparent that the only way a computerised stock system can meet its main objectives is by integrating it with purchase ordering to indicate what is on order, sales order processing to indicate what has been ordered by customers, and sales invoicing in order to bring stock movements up to date more promptly.

If stock movement can be quickly recorded, then reporting on such things as low stock levels, general stock movements and trends, price changes, valuations and stock lists can be easily and efficiently carried out.

Implementing such a system can be as complicated as selecting the software and installing it; an issue which will be discussed later.

Payroll

Payroll, as an application, was one of the earliest business tasks for which a computer was used. Typically, many firms, then and now, used an outside agency (such as Computer Bureau) to process a payroll run on a weekly or monthly basis. Firms send details of employees' work and sickness for each payment period together with details of any new employees and information on employees who are leaving. After a few days the firm receives payment details for each employee. Even with an outside agency operating a company payroll system, work is still required in order to get details to the agency. Such agencies are often well geared up to handle a large variety of payroll systems and can often offer a cheaper solution to the payroll problem than a firm can achieve by running its own.

The essence of payroll is to pay staff a wage or salary in much the same way as paying for any other commodity or service. In fact, wages and salaries are treated as an expense to the firm and, as any other business expense, will accordingly appear in the nominal ledger.

To justify computerising payroll for a business there has to be, realistically, a large number of employees; usually more than a dozen. It will take considerable cost and effort to set the system up, to learn it and to use and administer it. It is unlikely, therefore, that a firm with fewer than about six people on its payroll can benefit from computerised payroll. A firm that employs casual staff can find a payroll application extremely useful.

With a larger number of employees, once the system has been set up the time saved can be quite considerable. In a manual system, the determination of PAYE, National Insurance and pension figures can be very tedious and time consuming. A computer can work through such calculations with ease and efficiency. Also the final documentation generated by computerised payroll should meet the requirements of the various bodies such as the Inland Revenue and Social Security Departments as well as the business's own accounting system.

Databases

A good deal of time and effort is spent in the computing industry discussing and developing what is described as *database software*. (To some extent, databases have already been covered in this chapter. Most accounting software, for example, is a form of database, albeit directed at a more specific application. Spreadsheets are also specialised databases.)

A database is a form of electronic filing system. Most businesses maintain a database in some form such as:

- A collection of customer or client details.
- A profile of products either sold or purchased.
- A collection of employee records.

A database holds units of data in what are known as records. In the customer file, you would find a record for each customer. These records are structured into fields. There would be one field for name, another for post code, another for current balance, etc. Another example, that of an employee record, is shown in Fig. 3.1. The figure shows a record structure made up of four fields with one record for each employee.

Employee file

Works no.	Employee name	Status	Address
0001/192	David Black	Packer	12 King St, Newtown
1992/782	Denise Blue	Supervisor	1 High St. Barntown
1200/122	John Green	Driver	10 Broadwalk, Plinstone
3410/333	Jane Yellow	Driver	5 Queen St, Newtown

Fig. 3.1 Extract from an employee file

Databases offer the user complete flexibility regarding the structure of records and the range of record types. It is possible to meet most of a business's information needs using a database package.

A database, therefore, is a formal way of storing information. A record could be a collection of facts about a product such as its name, its price and the names of suppliers. On the other hand, a database might also hold a list of records about the sales of the stock such as who bought it, the price at which it was sold, the number of units sold.

From a business point of view, you will need to decide whether a general database package would be suitable, or whether you need one more closely related to the needs of your business. One of the requirements of a database package such as dBase or Dataease is that you will need to decide on what records are required, how they are to be structured and any relationships between differing record types that are required. You will find that the development of a database system using database software is a skilled job in its own right. It is possible for business people to produce simple applications with databases, but their time would normally be better spent with their businesses than trying to produce a solution to a complex problem with databases.

The situation may arise where the only way to meet a business's information needs is to use a database package and pay for someone to develop the database program to meet those needs. The problem with this is an obvious one: it will prove both costly and time consuming. It is often better to buy a ready-made application package which can be inexpensive and quick to implement.

Bill of materials

A bill of materials is effectively an extension of a stock control system. It examines the way some stock is actually used. In a manufacturing firm, a product may be manufactured using components held in stock. In other words, a group of components taken from stock are used in order to create a single product, or even a part for another product. The concept of bill of materials is to record the types and numbers of components that are used to create assemblies, an assembly being a composition of components. The computer, therefore, treats an assembly *record* as a collection of component *fields*. This is often referred to as an *explosion record*, since the assembly is separated into its components.

One of the benefits of the bill of materials is that it simplifies the determination of the cost of work-in-progress by valuing stock currently being used to assemble products.

An important feature of the bill of materials is the possibility of interaction with the ordering procedures and the stock control to ensure that stock is available to meet orders. It can inform users of quantities of stock that are required to meet future commitments. As the assembly proceeds, the system must take out of stock and place into work-in-progress all those components that are required to make the finished products. Apart from being a major time saving facility, the computerised bill of materials system is also a useful tool for assessing a firm's manufacturing potential at any given time.

Job costing

For many firms the use of the ledgers will prove insufficient for either controlling or monitoring costs. Instead, they may decide to analyse cost by job or department. For example, a building contractor will wish to control the costs and assess the profitability of a number of projects. In addition to monitoring profits, the analysis of costs will assist companies in realistically assessing the costs of new projects and, as a consequence, enable them to compete with other building firms for contracts.

Alternatively, a firm may break its operations down into cost centres or departments and will then wish to monitor costs of such departments, assess their performance and measure their profitability. As transactions are generated in terms of acquisition of goods, services, materials and wages paid, the costs are then allocated to the jobs.

Job cost reports are extracted indicating costs of each job, project or departmental activity.

In order for job costing to be effective, it requires details of costs from some of the other functions to be collected from the accounting system. Consequently, job costing requires integration with other functions. By implication, therefore, job costing tends to be an extension of an accounting system rather than a stand alone application. Most firms, therefore, will tend to phase this activity in after their accounting system has been developed.

3

Communications

Data communications is a specialist area that small businesses new to computing are unlikely to get much involved with. You will often see this area of technology described as DataComms or simply Comms.

Data communications is about getting data from one point to another by electronic means in rather the same say as a telephone works. In fact, most data communicating will be done through a telephone line. For most users, such communications will be used for one of the following:

1. **To have a computer gain access to a public database such as British Telecom's Prestel or BT Gold.**
2. **To get two computers on different sites to pass information between them.**
3. **To expand a computer network to allow a terminal to be set up far away from the file server and act as a remote job entry (RJE) station.**

For whatever purpose you wish to use data communications, you will almost certainly require a *modem* (modulator/demodulator) device that is attached to your computer or a communications card that fits into your machine. If it is certain that you will need this technology, then you should purchase a computer with the required attachments. In addition to this hardware, you will need the prerequisite software. Again, you will need to be careful to specify exactly what you want from data communications in order to be certain to get the correct software.

Graphics and design

Graphics capabilities of computers are largely dependent upon the hardware as well as the software. Therefore, if you are to use computers for a graphics application, it is necessary to ensure that the need is identified early on so that the correct hardware is acquired. If the hardware is wrong for graphics, it will have to be upgraded, and upgrading a machine can be more expensive than buying correctly in the first place. This fact reinforces the need for users to identify their software needs before embarking on *any* purchasing.

In order to run a graphics based package you will need a machine that can address a graphics screen (as opposed to a text orientated one) and a screen of sufficient resolution that allows graphical displays of a suitable quality for your application. The sophistication of the hardware is again dependent upon the nature of the graphics application. Desk top publishing, as mentioned earlier, can make extensive use of graphics for digitising photographic images and displaying a range of type fonts in differing sizes.

Another major application for graphics is in the area of design. Both technical and engineering drawing can benefit from computer technology. The precision and accuracy that can be achieved by computers can be very high. Computers have the ability to store and retrieve all or sections of drawings. The combination of standard components is made very simple and in many cases can be automated and optimised according to predetermined criteria. Such technology is relatively expensive when compared to such applications as word processing or accounts because of the complicated nature of both the hardware and the software.

There is a large number of modest, but useful, graphics packages available on the market not requiring expensive computing equipment. Such packages are useful for such applications as stationery design and producing simple picture-based output. It is important for a business that wishes to use such an application to be clear about the quality of printed output needed. For better quality output a laser printer might be required, although most matrix printers are capable of printing graphics output. If direct colour output is required then this will add to the cost and sophistication of the hardware, although it is worthwhile investigating multi-pen plotters and colour ink-jet printers.

Some software accessories

A whole host of useful and cheap (or even free) software packages are available that often come bundled with hardware or other software applications, such as calendars and diaries for keeping appointments and assisting you in determining working days in a month. In practice, such software tools can be very useful.

Calculators are also available and some software packages such as word processors and accounts packages have calculators built into them. Again, these tools are useful as they allow you to work with complex calculations and formulae and even to store the sequences of operations so that you can repeat the work with different values.

Clocks and timing devices can often be displayed in the corner of your screen to help you watch the hours disappear as you get wrapped up in your computer work. Some programs of this nature have an alarm clock built in that can be made to beep at a specified time.

There is an abundance of utilites and novelties available, with more coming onto the market all the time. You cannot get to know them all, and very few of them will be of direct use to business. Many such programs often come free with magazines.

Integrated software

The idea of integrated packages was mentioned earlier, with specific references to accounts and business applications. Integrated accounts is an obvious and useful form of integrating applications to the point that it can almost be regarded as a single application rather than a collection of different applications.

There are many applications that integrate word processing, spreadsheet, database, business graphics and communications. Benefits can arise from buying such a package because it might be able to supply all your computer solutions at once.

The obvious benefit is that it should prove cheaper than buying each application separately. In addition to this, integrated packages mean that you only have *one* package to learn instead of many; and only one set of documentation to worry about. Integrated packages often mean that transfer of data between applications is much easier; e.g. spreadsheet data can be easily transferred to the word processor.

An important benefit of integrated packages is that the key strokes on the keyboard and the way in which each application works tend to be very similar. This can be extremely useful as even experts tend to slow down in their operations when moving from one package to another that has been developed by a different company.

Integrated software can have its problems. There is the danger that integrating applications in this way means you end up with a package that is a 'Jack of all trades and a master of none'. For many businesses, however, their needs may be such that they do not need all the facilities offered by a highly sophisticated package dedicated to a single application. Another problem that may arise is that for a new user integrated software can appear overwhelming and too much to learn in one go. Such packages can, of course, be learnt one module at a time, but it is unlikely that tuition for them would come cheap.

Standardising software

Standardising software is not easy to achieve because very few software firms produce a wide enough range to meet all of a business's needs. What we mean by standardising software is that you acquire software from the same source or from sources that are coordinated in some way by, say, a hardware manufacturer. The main benefit is that the philosophy adopted by a software firm tends to be carried across all of that firm's products. The practical benefit of this is that key strokes are similar for similar operations.

Sampling software

Being able to sample software before you commit your business to using it is always to be recommended if possible. There are a number of ways this can be done:

---

1. **Viewing the software already implemented in another business. Seeing a package in action in a real situation has the obvious advantage of showing you its capabilities. Thought, however, needs to be given to whether the package is suitable for your own business.**
2. **Receiving a demonstration from a vendor. This can be quite effective, although a vendor may not be willing to allow this if a substantial sale is not likely. Some vendors, however, will**

allow a demonstration if it is done on their premises.

   If you use a small firm of consultants, then they should be able to set up a demonstration of the software they have chosen for your business to give you a better idea of what can be achieved. Also, the use of consultants tends to place the onus on them to ensure you are exposed to the correct software.
3. Attending an exhibition. Exhibitions can be difficult for people to get to, and then are inclined to be very technical and unlikely to give you, a new potential user, a real insight into what the software can do for your business. However, they can offer an introduction to what is available.
4. Examination of the software with a distribution disk. Many software producers distribute free disks giving some insight into the capabilities and workings of a package. One problem with this is that you will need a computer in order to see it. Another is that the manufacturer will be showing the product off to its best advantage and it might not come up to expectations when you get a full working copy.
5. Attending a course. This may appear to be a little drastic if all you want to do is to get an appreciation of a single package. In practice, attending a course will be of more benefit if you are learning a package that you have decided to commit your business to.

What do you get in a software package?

With your software package you will normally receive:

1. A set of disks (the software).
2. An installation guide. Application packages are often written for a number of machines with different configurations. The purpose of installing a package is to adapt it to a specific machine. Often this gives the supplier an opportunity to ensure that you register the product as a legal version. Businesses will want to use packages in different ways, and installing a package will allow a business to tailor it a little more closely to its own needs.
3. A reference manual. These can often be long and technical in nature, but will represent full and comprehensive documentation on what your package can do and how it does it.
4. A tutorial. This often combines written notes with software and provides basic introduction concerning the use of the

package. Tutorials rarely cover all aspects of what the
package can do but serve as a useful starting point for those
going it alone with applications software.
5. Registration and promotions literature.

The problem of obsolescence

Many software packages soon become out of date or even obsolete.
Often this is not a serious problem; while hardware and software
are doing a job efficiently, there is little point in making alterations
simply to keep up with what is available on the market.

Even so, most software producers recognise the fact that many
users like to keep abreast of the latest developments. If you purchase
a package and find that a later version becomes available, you will
often be given an opportunity to trade it in for the newer version
at a nominal fee. Such offers are often available for a few months only.

Not taking advantage of upgrades could leave you with a problem
of having software that your supplier will no longer support, as the
supplier will normally only support the upgraded version.

You will need to consider that software can become quickly
obsolete because your own business needs will change or because
legislation changes the way information has to be collated or changes
business practices.

Summary

We began this chapter by considering what we want from a computer. In other words, what can the computer do for your business? The software market offers a number of well established applications including:

- Word processing and desk top publishing.
- Spreadsheets.
- Database.
- Accounts and payroll.
- Stock control.
- Communications.
- Graphics.

You should decide on the kind of applications your business needs.

   If you require a range of software products, then it is always worth considering the possibility of standardising on similar products to make the operating and learning of a package easier.

   Before buying, try to sample your software.

   As a final point, the use of an independent consultant can prove an invaluable investment. If you find yourself with the wrong software, you can end up with a computer that fails to do the job you want, or miss out on the real potential of computerisation.

3

4 Getting started with your computer

Staff training □ Installing software and preparing disks □ Converting your information for the computer □ Setting up computer files □ Testing software □ Phasing in □ Establishing procedures and methods □ Computer system maintenance

One of the most difficult aspects of using a computerised system is the process of setting it up. In most businesses, transactions are being carried out on a very regular basis and details about such things as stock quantities and customer accounts are difficult to compile accurately at any given point of time. When setting up a computer system, we will have to enter all the details about the state of a business before we can start using the system. The problem here is that by the time all the required information has been compiled and entered, it has become out of date. This problem is the classical one of trying to hit a moving target!

This issue will be raised in this chapter, with ideas about how to overcome some of the problems and dilemmas facing a firm wishing to computerise a manual system while continuing to operate it.

When implementing a computer system, time and patience are required. Computerising a manual system *cannot* be done overnight; it may well take weeks or months. In Chapters 7 and 12 there are case studies which will put a lot of this into perspective and offer a much better analysis of implementing computer systems.

For now, we shall consider the main issues.

Staff training

One of the first and key steps in developing a computerised system is to ask: 'Are the staff adequately prepared and trained?' The success of the system will depend upon the answer. All too often firms have wasted valuable time and money because operators simply do not know how to use key software properly, look after equipment, carry out the correct operational procedures, troubleshoot or back up.

There are a number of ways of ensuring that the staff who have to operate a computerised system are trained; some of them are:

---

1. Purchase a system and the required software from a firm which also offers staff training. This is the most likely way to be certain that training is directly related to the system implemented. If you are using a standard commercial package such as an accounts package or word processing package, it is unlikely that the supplying firm will offer direct training.

   The kind of training that a supplier might offer will relate to operating the computer itself, such as:

   - Powering up the system.
   - Shutting the system down.
   - Backing up data.
   - Cleaning and general preventive maintenance.
   - Performing some of the operating system commands.
   - Changing and using disks.

   A supplier may, however, employ a third party to ensure that operators get training on some of the applications software, especially if it was requested in an original specification.

2. Send a member of staff on a course. Such courses are available at various times of the year from both private institutions and local colleges. Your problem is likely to be finding a course in the right place at the right time.

   Private institutions are normally specially geared up for certain applications and run courses at their own centres. Courses at your own site can sometimes be arranged.

   Technical colleges and polytechnics are now becoming more aware of the potential of commercial training and it would be well worth your while inquiring about what they might have on offer.

3. Employ someone who is already trained. This may not be an option, and even if it is it should still be remembered that employing someone with computer expertise does not necessarily mean they adapt to your company methods without training.

   Once your system has become well established and a vacancy arises, you will need to consider computer expertise when recruiting staff. It is worth mentioning that computer expertise in the employment market is generally in

4

short supply. Even when you recruit new staff, you may
have no option but to put them through considerable
training before you can use them effectively.
4. Hope that an employee can learn the package and computer
system as they implement it, giving them time to research
and experiment. Although this option is extremely risky, it is
often used.

Staff training is an expense of implementing a computer system
often overlooked by firms. Poorly trained staff can lead to the
downfall of *any* system, not just a computerised one.

Installing software and preparing disks

When software is purchased, it may arrive on a number of disks
ready to be transferred to your own hard disk. With the disks will
come a whole set of documents of which one will be an installation
guide.

If you have given yourself the job of installing your own software,
then you will need to follow the installation instructions carefully.
This exercise can be very time consuming for a novice and prone
to errors; we would advise that the job is done by your supplier
as part of the service provided.

Application packages are often written for a number of machines
with varying configurations. The purpose of installing a package
is to adapt it to a specific machine. For instance, some machines
use colour output and others do not; some installations software
has to be installed on a hard disk rather than floppy disks.

Businesses will want to use packages in different ways, and
installing a package will allow the business to tailor it a little more
closely to its own needs.

Converting your information for the computer

It is almost certain that if you are converting from a manual system
to a computer system, the way in which your information is organised
will have to alter. If, for example, you are computerising your sales
ledger, then customer details will have to be collected and compiled
appropriately before you can start using the computer.

Gathering such information can be a difficult job in its own right.

Many customer files, for example, are 'active'. In other words, they are tied up in another person's office or even off the premises.

Before collecting and compiling the information required, you will be best advised to study the relevant software in order to establish exactly what you need to build up the system and the information required by the computer.

Once the information has been gathered in this way, you will have to act quickly to get it onto the computer and running before it becomes too outdated to use. Carrying out this activity can have some unforeseen benefits. Quite often it gives a business the opportunity of having a good 'clear out' and discovering lost information. Also, you can use this exercise as an opportunity to get yourself better organised. For example, most stock control systems on computers require minimum stock and stock reorder levels. This may make you think carefully about what stock levels are desirable in your company. Also, such an application often requires details like lead times (the time it takes to receive the goods once the order has been placed).

Another major activity that will normally have to be undertaken is *coding*. Nearly all business and accounting information systems will require a coding system; this may, or may not, match your current system of coding. Three examples will illustrate this:

---

1. **Stock control will require you to assign a unique code to each item of stock. You should think very carefully about this, because once a system is set up and running, changing a coding system can be just as time consuming and awkward as setting up the system in the first place.**

   The business will normally have the opportunity of devising a coding system to suit its own needs, such as relating a code to the location of stock on the premises, or to the supplier.

   In supermarkets, all products are coded and the codes are represented by bar codes on the products. Although we would not suggest you use bar coding systems, the example does at least stress the importance businesses attach to such codes.

2. **If you are computerising your purchasing system, then each supplier should have a code attached to it, i.e. a supplier code. These codes could be used to reveal something about the suppliers, such as their reliability or location. When applying codes, you should note that each supplier code must be unique and that you will not be able to change it once implemented.**

Likewise, the sales ledger will contain transaction details for each customer. Each customer must again have a unique code, normally called an account number or customer reference number.

3. With a payroll system, each employee will have to be given a unique identification code, normally called a payroll number or works number. Although two employees can have exactly the same name, no two employees can have the same payroll number. Such codes can reveal information about the employees such as the department they work in, when they were first employed or the pay scale they are on. If the status of the employee changes, then you might have to close the employee's records and create another payroll number. Most payroll packages give you an easy way to transfer details from one number to another.

There are numerous examples where such coding is needed, and businesses often take this opportunity to restructure their information systems.

Although the emphasis in this discussion has been on allocating numbers (1, 2, 3 . . .) to everything, in practice nearly all codes are either numeric or alphabetic (A, B, C . . .) or a combination of both (alphanumeric, A1, A12/23C).

Whatever the coding system used, there is no escaping the fact that whoever is responsible for devising the methods must know both the software and the business system. Again, we hark back to the fact that selection of software and staff training in the use of the software will be the keys to the success of running the computerised system.

Setting up computer files

Once the information has been collected and collated, you will need to get it onto the computer promptly; while you are putting the information onto the computer, activities within the business will already be causing some of it to be out of date. The situation could arise, therefore, that as soon as you have got the information onto the computer, another major job needs to be done to bring it all back up to date. It would be rather like painting the Forth Bridge.

You will require help doing this if your own staffing resources cannot cope. Where possible, most small businesses will rely on their own staff working extra hours rather than employing casual staff to help them out.

This file conversion activity can offer staff very useful training and help them become more aware of the business operations.

Where possible, there is a good deal to be gained by phasing in computerisation across business areas as and when ready. This will leave you with lots of small manageable problems to solve rather than one big unmanageable problem. More will be said about this later.

Testing software

The chances are, the software you use will be 'off the shelf'; it will have been well proven in the market place and be free of what we call 'bugs'. A program bug is something that makes it go wrong. What you are more likely to be testing at this stage is your understanding of the package and the way it has been installed. Also, in the early days of running a computerised system, there will always be teething problems where you are not doing things correctly. If staff have been well trained, then the probability is that there will be far fewer and less important errors in operation than if staff are poorly trained.

Phasing in

The questions will be:

1. **Do we convert to the computerised system in one go?**
2. **Do we phase in computerisation over a period of time?**
3. **Do we run both computer and manual systems until we have got the computer system running properly?**
4. **Do we do some kind of combination of the above?**

This issue is worth thinking about now, and will also be raised in the case studies in Chapters 7 and 12. In Part 4 we will tackle this question in some detail.

Establishing procedures and methods

A good deal of attention will have to be paid to the need for a disciplined approach to maintaining the system and files so that regular running is ensured, updated files are maintained and users are kept in touch. As you will find, running a computer system is still very much like running any manual system in that once you have established routine procedures you should stick to them.

One of the benefits to be derived from having a computer is the ease and efficiency with which it can extract reports and get hold of information. Such information will only be of real practical use if it is kept up to date. For example, if you are running your ledgers on the computer, you should be able to extract any information about a customer account in just a few seconds. If customer orders, payments and invoices are not being processed early on then the information you are extracting is out of date and fails to inform you correctly. Likewise, if a stock control system does not record movements soon after they happen, then you will not get an accurate reflection of stock levels and could find yourself either running out of stock or reordering stock that has already been ordered.

Although transactions should be placed onto the computer soon after they happen, you have to avoid a situation where an operator runs to the computer every time an invoice appears, an item of stock is issued or a bill is received. You will need to use common sense in deciding how to batch your work in such a way that:

- too much time is not spent by operators preparing documents for data input to the computer;
- time is not wasted going through the process of setting up the machine for applications in order to enter just a few transactions;
- information on the computer is not out of date and misleading.

You will need to organise a system where certain documents, such as incoming invoices, are batched until there are sufficient to warrant the time to place the information onto the computer.

In some cases, you may want to place information onto the computer immediately a transaction occurs. If, for example, you need to keep stock details up to date by the minute, then an operator will have to place the details onto the computer at the crucial moment. If this is to be the case, then it is important that it is established early on in the development process. It may necessitate, for example, having a computer terminal in the warehouse so that the person issuing or receiving stock can enter the transaction straightaway, rather than having to fill in movement sheets and later having an operator put the details into the computer; after all, one of the purposes of having a computer system is to eliminate the need for duplicating the entry of information details.

Establishing procedures may, therefore, include:

- setting times in the week when invoices are processed.
- setting times in the week when sales orders are processed.
- setting up a procedure for issuing stock.
- deciding on what reports should be regularly produced and at what times in the week and to which people copies should be supplied.
- establishing a method for purchase ordering.

The list can go on indefinitely and will, in most businesses, be subject to constant review.

You will probably find yourself very quickly drawing parallels between the computer based system and your old manual one. This is how it should be. Once a computer system has settled and is functioning well, it may well be seen that the procedures have not really changed in principle but the technology has.

Computer system maintenance

More will be said about this in Part 4, but for now a few points should be made.

Losing data on a computer is really no different from losing your paper work: it could be fatal. With computers there are a whole host of things that could go wrong. If your data is properly *backed up* you should have nothing to fear and should be able to sleep at night that much better.

Acquiring and implementing a computer system

Part 2 focuses attention on the actual purchasing decision. It helps you to decide what tasks the computer should perform when it is initially installed, and what additional tasks it might be used for in the future.

It discusses where to get specific advice on such matters, and then it goes on to discuss what to buy and where to buy it.

You will find that Appendix 5 at the end of the book contains useful supplementary checklists to help you when preparing a tender document.

Part 2 also discusses the cost structure, including both initial costs and running costs, as well as direct system costs and hidden costs such as time and future training. Before you examine costs in greater detail, Chapter 7 offers you a case study as a means of placing much of this into context.

5 Initial costs of computerisation

Direct computer costs □ The hidden or indirect costs □ Assessing costs against the benefits

This chapter will attempt to identify the actual costs of computerisation. This will enable you to go some way towards measuring such costs, while showing you that a sizeable proportion of the costs of computing are 'hidden'. Businesses should not be carried away by the well advertised fact that the real costs of computer hardware and software are falling.

5

Direct computer costs

When discussing direct costs, we refer to those costs that can be readily attributed to computerisation. Because such costs are normally very easy to identify, they are also easier to control.

Direct costs can be broken down into two distinct areas. First, there are those costs that come about from the time a computer system is proposed to the day it is installed and running. Second, there are those costs that carry on over the lifetime of the computer system such as running costs.

Direct immediate costs

A direct immediate cost is the actual total cost of buying and implementing a computer and will generally have a definite time limit imposed on it. The sums comprising this total will have to be financed almost straightaway as it tends to be these costs that will cause most immediate concern. Of the costs covered in this chapter, the direct costs will probably be the easiest to measure. Even so, they can escalate beyond what has been budgeted for; it is wise to allow a little more in the budget to cover any extras that may be overlooked.

Hardware

The cost of hardware is the most obvious short term direct cost. A good deal of public attention has, of course, been focused on the fact that hardware costs have been continually falling while the power and capabilities of computers have been increasing. Without a doubt this has meant that it has become feasible to apply computerised techniques in small businesses as well as in larger businesses, corporations and public bodies.

One of the problems faced by many users is that caused by the pace of technological change. The dilemma is whether to buy now or wait for new improvements to come onto the market. We did suggest that you will nearly always be able to upgrade software to newer versions at a nominal fee because software firms are anxious not to put users into a 'wait and see' situation. This is less likely to happen with hardware.

Unless you are a computer enthusiast, you would be ill advised to adopt a 'wait and see' policy. As the situation stands at the moment with the rapid developments in computers available on the market, we have to be realistic and argue that this is a decision you will never get right; in five years your acquisition will show signs of becoming outdated. The financial implication of this is that you can probably depreciate the asset by 20 per cent of the cost price per annum on the basis of obsolescence alone. Remember, this is no more than you would depreciate on a new company car – is it?

The emphasis of your policy on computer acquisition should always be on whether the system can perform the tasks of the business and be capable of being maintained rather than whether you can keep pace with the latest technological developments.

Software

Short term costs will go beyond actual hardware; software must also be considered. Software costs can vary considerably and it is very easy to find yourself paying too much for software.

If you are purchasing standard application packages, then it is always worth shopping around if you have given yourself the job of purchasing the software (you may well have commissioned the vendor to undertake that job when you requested a quote and proposal on a complete computer system).

If software has to be specially written or adapted for your business needs (sometimes called 'bespoke software'), then the cost could well escalate quite considerably.

A good deal of software will often be included with the hardware and so it is not easy to distinguish software costs from the other costs. Nearly all systems include the operating system with its required documentation. Many systems also come with some applications software such as desk top utilities and word processors. Be careful not to allow yourself to be persuaded to buy a system that does not match your business requirements just because you are offered supposedly free software.

Overall, it is not unusual to find that software costs exceed the hardware costs.

Installation and cabling

The cost of installation and cabling can vary considerably depending on the type of system being employed. A network of computers will generate higher costs than one or more stand alone machines. Such costs will normally be quoted to you in a vendor's proposal.

Staff training

With the advent of a new computer system will come the need for new skills. The need for staff training has already been covered, but it will constitute new costs to the business.

Some staff training may come as part of a 'package' deal from a vendor and so cannot be costed in isolation. If third parties are being used then the costs will become apparent. Such training is normally costed on a daily basis, with the length of the course depending upon the computer application.

Staff costs must also include the cost of a member of staff not being available to do normal duty. Such a cost can be easy to measure if you have to pay overtime for staff getting work loads completed, but it becomes more difficult if work left has caused delays in deliveries and orders being processed.

Staffing for conversion

During the process of preparing information for computerisation and actually getting such information into the computer, a good deal of human effort and time will be spent. The costs will tend to be paid in overtime and bonus payments to staff.

Maintenance and support contracts

With a new system a contract that ensures emergency repair or cover in the event of a system breakdown or failure is always worthwhile in the first two years of a system's lifetime. After this, you will have to assess the contracts to see if they are worth renewing.

Environmental costs

Such costs may be negligible depending on the type of system being used. However, in some cases computers do need a change of environment from the one offered by the business. More on this will be covered in Part 3.

Direct long term costs

We now direct our attention to those costs which, in varying degrees of importance and magnitude, will occur after you have got your system fully operational. Such costs will be very difficult to measure but many firms budget for computing expenditure from year to year. As will be mentioned, some uncertainty can be removed through maintenance and service contracts and insurance.

Maintenance and repair

Maintenance and repair have already been mentioned as short term costs. However, if you do not take out a maintenance contract on a longer term basis then repair costs may well be incurred later.

Even if a contract is agreed, the time will come when it runs out. You may decide to renew the contract if you believe that it is worth renewing. Make sure that all such contracts are reviewed regularly. It is possible to be paying more in maintenance contract costs than your system is actually worth, in which case it would be cheaper to replace your system. Some contracts are broken down according to the parts of the computer covered and the amount paid for each, such as maintenance of printers, computer's system and cabling. In this case the merits of each part of the contract should be examined separately.

If you do take out maintenance contracts, then be careful about what is actually covered. For example, if your printers were to break down, are you covered or do you have to pay for special repairs? Also, does maintenance include parts and equipment?

Remember, you can always live without any contract at all and pay for repairs and maintenance as and when needed. If, as a business, you employ someone with technical expertise, then there seems little point in having a full-blown maintenance contract; a good insurance policy would be more useful.

Maintenance contracts will normally cover you for hardware only. If anything happens to your software then you will find yourself coping with a different problem.

Accessories

Computer accessories will cover a whole range of things but will be an ongoing cost of running a computer system.

Printers will need replacement of their ribbons in much the same way that a typewriter would. It is always wise to keep at least one spare ribbon per printer.

Printers also require paper. Although nearly all printers will accept single sheets of paper, they are often designed to accept continuous paper. The benefit of this is that you do not need to change paper each time a sheet has been filled – important when printing a large number of invoices or a stock listing. Such stationery can be readily purchased from a number of stationers dealing in computer supplies. Also such stationery can be produced with your business logo on it for such things as invoices or statements, and can be two, three or four part stationery. In practice, of course, you will probably need this stationery whether you have a computer system or not.

Special cleaning equipment should be purchased such as anti-static sprays to keep display screens clean and special disk head cleaning kits to keep your disk drive clean.

Replacement disks and tapes may also be needed. Over time you may wish to save transactions information on such storage media. You will find yourself running out over time, and although disks and tapes are re-usable, they do not have an infinite life.

Staff training and development

Staff training and development should be an ongoing exercise for a business and you may well wish to attend training courses or put your staff on such courses in order to learn about new products or improve on existing skills.

If you recruit new staff to operate the system, then they may well have to attend training courses.

Replacement of equipment

When you get an equipment failure, such as a broken visual display screen or a printer, you will probably need to replace it. Disks and various components inside the computer itself may also be subject to failure and need replacing.

Upgrading

Although it is likely that, whatever system you end up with, there will always be technology on the market that is more up to date, there will always be the opportunity of buying in upgrades in order to take advantage of these changes.

You may decide that a new model of printer will enhance your output and the extra investment is justified. In this instance, be careful that you do not encounter an unwanted 'knock on' effect in that in order to use the new printer you need to radically alter your software and the stationery that you use.

Some upgrades are needed in order to take advantage of a new software product; there may not be enough room on your disk to support it or there may be insufficient memory to run your program.

General development costs

In time, you may well wish to develop your system further. Once you have mastered some major business activities you may find yourself computerising other business data processing functions, all of which may require extra computing resources.

The danger of developing in this way is that in order for a system to cope, it may need to be radically altered. This would be unfortunate; it implies that at the planning stage early on such development had not been foreseen.

You may decide, for example, to allow other users in your business access to the computer's information, and so would look to add on extra computers to a network or extra terminals to a multi-user. Alternatively, if you operate on more than one site, you may decide to set up a computer station on another site using data communications equipment to relay data down telephone wires.

All such developments should be within the scope of businesses and will be discussed in Part 4.

The hidden or indirect costs

These costs can cause some of the greatest anguish to businesses – not because of the amount involved, but because much of it has not been budgeted for from the outset. Many of the hidden costs will go unnoticed even though they are adding to the expense of the business.

Paying for greater skills

Having built up your system and developed your staff to a level of competency that enables them to master the system well, you should bear in mind that there is a good chance you are now employing much sought-after staff. If your staff do not insist on extra salary for acquiring such skills, there is a good chance that they may be tempted into jobs where their skills are better rewarded.

Also, when the time comes to recruit new staff, some of the posts will require staff with computing expertise. Such staff will only come forward if you are willing to pay a premium for their skills. If you take on staff without these skills you will have to pay to get them trained.

Whatever the situation, you will find only one long term solution to maintaining a competent and well trained staff – pay them more.

Even though you may find yourself paying staff more than you might otherwise without a computer system, you should bear in mind that by virtue of having a computerised system, your business offers the kind of career prospects that good quality staff often seek.

Conditions of service

There will be considerable changes to business procedures and methods as a result of employing computerised techniques. Such changes will result in changes of conditions of service. You will need to bear this in mind throughout the duration of such a project. It is always wise to keep staff actively involved where possible and informed at all times. Labour disputes can be very costly and frustrating to a system's development.

Learning time

It is surprising how much time is spent at keyboards, learning the system or simply experimenting with the computer. The cost of such time is difficult to assess, but sometimes we have to ask ourselves whether the time spent could not have been put to better use.

However, we would hope that a good deal of time is spent getting access to information; being able to spend time interrogating your business information database will help you make more prudent and rational business decisions.

Furniture

Buying computer equipment will often result in operators needing changes in furniture, such as somewhere to put the printer so that the paper feeds in and out of it correctly, getting a desk so that the keyboard and screen are in a better position, or chairs that make it more comfortable to operate a computer. A situation will often arise where either you or an operator simply do not have enough room on the desk to fit a computer. These needs are not only important from a comfort point of view, there is also a health and safety matter to consider.

Another requirement for extra furniture may come about because you need somewhere to store things such as disks and stationery.

You will find no shortage of literature and catalogues offering to sell you appropriate furniture. A good deal of money can be saved by 'shopping' around for good deals.

Software support

This is more likely to be applicable to those who have software written for them or specially tailored. As the business develops its systems, it will often find that its software needs to be adapted to meet the changing circumstances. Before you realise it you are paying out extra development costs to have your software changed.

In many cases you may find you need to make unexpected changes to general software. For example, each year (and sometimes more often than yearly) government budgets will alter certain taxes such as rates of Pay As You Earn or National Insurance. Changes will need to be made within your software at the appropriate time. In fact, some changes may mean alterations in the structure of the software. In order to make such changes, professional help may be required at a cost to the business.

Another example would be if changes were made in the rates of VAT. This would have implications across a whole range of business applications software.

Most packages are flexible enough to allow changes such as those in taxation, and you can make the necessary adaptations yourself if you have gained sufficient knowledge of the packages.

Obsolescence

Obsolescence will tend to catch up with most business computer systems at some time in the future. With the rapid changes being made within this technology and the supporting software that goes with it, obsolescence could set in after only a few years.

Although you can always go on running your system while it is still functioning, there is the real problem of the market place not supporting it. For example, it may become difficult to acquire ribbons for very old printers, or new programs for the older range of computers. This can be a serious problem because it simply leaves a company standing alone with what begins to look like old technology.

It is very difficult to say at this point what the future holds, but there is a good chance that after about five years, changes may have to be made in order to bring systems a little more up to date. In practice, you may well find yourself developing simply to avoid any major changes.

Even when obsolescence sets in, you will not necessarily need to scrap all your equipment and replace it with new.

Insurance

With extra resources being employed by the business, your insurance costs are likely to rise.

Do not allow the fact that your computing resources are insured to lull you into a false sense of security. A more serious loss than that of equipment is that of the business's information, which cannot be insured in the same way. There will *never* be a better insurance policy than the effective backing up of information.

Changes in the law

Sudden changes in the law can cause problems for computer users, such as changes in tax laws or employment laws or accounting practices.

The only really significant change in the law so far has been the Data Protection Act, which is outlined in Appendix 2 at the end of this book.

Assessing costs against the benefits

There will always be a cost to computerising any function. The aim will, of course, be to minimise costs while maximising the benefits to be gained. An understanding of the likely costs should assist the business in budgeting.

The costs outlined in this chapter will vary according to the nature of the business concerned, its size and the type of system being used. In Chapter 8 we shall return to the issue of the costs of computerisation once you have gained an appreciation of what is involved in setting yourself up and have examined a case study as a way of placing much of this into context.

6 Your first steps to computerisation

Getting quotes from potential suppliers □ Specifying your needs □ A sample request □ Choosing a vendor □ Waiting for replies □ Making a comparison

Getting quotes from potential suppliers

Having established what you want from the computer and the general software you feel appropriate to your business needs, it is a good idea to put such details in writing and send them to a number of potential suppliers to see what they can offer.

As an alternative method to sending written specifications to potential suppliers, you can always search your *Yellow Pages* and make a few phone calls. Another possibility is to call into a shop that specialises in computer systems. However, both of these techniques can lead to quite a few problems.

One problem arising from personally asking vendors to quote specifications and costs is the difficulty of being able to make realistic comparisons between what they can offer your business. To ensure you can make a balanced comparison you will need to ensure that:

- Each vendor has been given sufficient information to assess your business computing needs.
- Each vendor has been given the *same* complete picture of your business. If a number of vendors are given different information, then you will get different feedback and will be unable to make a genuine comparison. In other words, you will be unable to compare like with like.

This second point really requires you to put your specifications in writing to a number of vendors. This would ensure that all vendors have the same information to work from. The quality of your feedback will only be as good as the information given. If, for example, you fail to inform a vendor that your computer system needs to allow up to four people to use it at the same time across a wide area, then it is unlikely that you will receive a quote for a system that supports this arrangement.

Specifying your needs

Your specification document should include the following information:

1. *The nature of the business*. This has implications for the kind of software that your business requires. For example, if your business is a travel agency, then there is already a good deal of software specifically written for travel agents that a vendor might want to examine. Likewise, if your business is that of a group of solicitors, there are numerous specialised software packages on the market available for such businesses. You should also include the nature of your markets, whether any overseas trade is done, the number of suppliers and customers, etc.
2. *An idea of the size of the business*. This helps vendors put your business into perspective, especially if they have experience in your kind of business area. As a guide, this information may include:

   - approximate turnover,
   - number of employees,
   - number of suppliers,
   - number of customers,
   - the types of documentation handled by the business and some idea of the volume involved, e.g. 500 invoices sent per month.

3. *What a computer would be expected to do*. You may not be absolutely certain at this stage. If you are not certain, you should say so. You may, however, have decided that word processing and ledger accounts are functions to be undertaken by the computer. Stating such information helps vendors to 'home in' quickly on some of the software requirements; they can put together a system more related to your requirements rather than what they think it should be. You may leave it to the vendor to decide if there are any other applications that your business could use. This makes sense because many vendors may already have experience of installing computer systems in businesses such as yours.
4. *The amount of information processing expected from a system*. It can be difficult to be precise about this, but it can

be assessed to a certain extent by an experienced vendor
from the size of your business and the amount of processing
you currently undertake. However, it will help if you can give
some idea about what volume of work has to be done and
how you see it changing in the foreseeable future.

5. *Current staffing.* Such information should include the number
of staff currently doing the work and approximately how
much time is spent on such processing activities.

6. *Current computing resources.* If you have any computing
equipment already in the business, it is worth stating this fact
as existing equipment can often be harnessed into a new
system.

7. *Preferences.* If you have any preferences for certain software
or hardware, then it is worth stating it in the tender
document. You might, for example, have a preference for one
accounting package because you are already familiar with it.
However, be careful not to put vendors into too much of a
straitjacket; it can quickly result in you not receiving a quote
and proposal on the optimum system for your business.

8. *Time scales.* You should say how soon you would hope to
see a system implemented, and whether you want it
implemented in one go or phased in over time. Time
constraints should always be realistic and if you are not sure
what a realistic time scale is, you can always leave it open to
suggestions from vendors; again, this fact should be stated.

9. *Budgets.* Many businesses will have some idea of how much
they expect to spend on hardware and software. It is normally
worth stating this amount in round figures so that you are not
wasting a vendor's or your own time. You can always state
that such a figure is a maximum rather than an actual amount
to spend.

10. *Setting a deadline.* This is a deadline by which you want a
quote delivered. You should be reasonable about this; a few
days is not long enough while (say) six months is too long. A
deadline of four to ten weeks depending on the sophistication
of the system required is quite long enough.

6

There is no reason, of course, why a more experienced person
cannot purchase a complete system through a magazine, catalogue
or high street shop and make a success of using it. However, without
any assurances of quality, professional help, advice and a second
opinion this could be risky.

For a checklist of the details that might appear on a tender
document, Appendix 5 at the end of this book should prove of
assistance to you.

A sample request

In order to give you some idea of how to approach a supplier, we shall give you an example of a specification sent to a vendor by a firm that imports sports equipment for resale.

To:

From:
Sports Supplies plc
200 London Road
Liverpool

21 August 19xx

Re: Business Computer System.

Dear Sirs,

We write to you as prospective suppliers of our new business computer system in the expectation that you will be able to supply us with a quote and proposal for the appropriate equipment. In order to assist you with producing a specification, we enclose some facts about the company together with details of our immediate computing needs.

Background

We are a private limited company managed and run by two directors. We have been trading for five years and have enjoyed continuous growth in sales over that period. Growth is projected for the next five years at approximately 10–15 per cent per annum.

The business specialises in the importation of sports equipment and the distribution of such goods to customers throughout the UK and Europe. Our sources are based mainly in the Far East, Pakistan and the United States and our range of products can include any kind of sports equipment depending on demand. We have found that there is no distinct pattern in the types of sales. For example, the sales of sports shoes and soccer balls have remained constant, while sales of squash rackets have grown constantly. Meanwhile sales of other products can be very erratic. The other problem faced by the company is that sales are influenced by seasonal factors; cricket and tennis related sports equipment sells well in summer while rugby and skiing related equipment sells well in autumn and winter.

The company has a turnover, at present, of about £2 million and employs eleven staff in the following areas: three warehouse staff, two full time clerical staff, two sales staff, two transport staff and two directors/managers. The company buys from up to thirty suppliers from twelve different countries.

Our sales effort is organised as follows:

1. There are fifteen agents who buy from the company. Ten are based around the UK and five in various parts of Europe.
2. We supply to five large chain stores: three in the UK, one in France and one in Luxembourg.
3. A small number of sales are made direct to sports clubs. Until now, this side of the business has not been encouraged to grow because the agents have done the work. Also, the company would find it difficult to cope with the volume of paper work that such sales would generate.

Our processing activities

With the growth in business activity that has been developed, we feel the time has now come to employ a computer system to handle a lot of the paper work. The company employs two clerical staff who are largely concerned with the general administration which includes:

1. Preparing invoices and statements of account for our customers. Up to thirty invoices are sent daily with all customers receiving statements at the end of each month. In many cases selling also requires the preparation of export documents.
2. Processing sales orders, up to thirty a day, has to be carried out as well.
3. As a result of large fluctuations in exchange rates, we are constantly updating our price lists. Our clerical staff are finding it difficult to cope with the problems this generates in keeping our customers informed and stocks properly valued.
4. Purchasing has a major role in our processing activities. This is a specialist job which requires market research and constant appraisal of our suppliers. This job is largely done by one of the directors but purchase orders are administered by the clerical staff.
5. Paying staff is also a responsibility of our clerical staff.

What we want from a computer

Having discussed this in some length, we feel that our immediate requirement for a computer is to meet the needs of points 1 and 2 outlined in our processing activities, with 3 and 4 following shortly after. We would expect a computer to be of assistance in the general processing of invoices, statements and orders as well as to be able to produce summaries to help us keep an eye on sales and movements of goods.

We also envisage that the system would manage our stock for us. Although it is largely left to the warehouse staff to decide what to order and when to order, we would want the computer to assist us in keeping much tighter control on stock so that we are neither left with unsold stock nor find ourselves running out of key products.

We feel payroll is of low priority to us as this does not take up too much time, but we might consider it as a longer term development.

One of our operators is well versed in word processing and has particular skills in the package Word Perfect. We would want, therefore, a specification to include word processing.

It is important that any proposed system allows *both* clerical staff as well as one of the managers to access it at the same time. If stock control is to be computerised as well, this might mean that warehouse staff also need access to the system.

Our computing skills

In short, very little.

As directors we have never really handled computers before and so have no preference for any particular system.

One of the clerical staff has attended a college course which, apart from word processing, involved her in training on applications software: namely Pegasus Business Software and Multiplan Spreadsheet. It has already been decided that any future system will be placed in her immediate charge.

We would like, therefore, any quote to include on-site training for both clerical staff, one director and possibly one other person.

Budget

We have no fixed budget to spend on a new system, but would envisage that it would not cost more than £20,000 in the first two years. We would very much hope that a good deal of the system would be up and running within eight months of a contract being drawn up.

We look forward to hearing from you in due course about a new computer system. If we have not heard from you six weeks after the date of this letter, we shall assume you are unable to give us a quote for the system.

Yours faithfully

Director

In practice, you may wish to be far more precise about the applications you feel appropriate for your business. Such an outline specification may still not be enough. Having started the process moving you yourself will at least have a much clearer idea of what you are looking for, and a vendor will have a very good idea what is required. A vendor may still want more information about your company and will probably make contact with you. For example, in order to arrive at the cost of hardware for this particular system, they may want to know something about the geography of your premises and where the proposed hardware is to be situated. Also there are such issues as:

- What kind of printer and how many are needed?
- Do you want colour screen output?
- Are the agents to get involved with the system?
- Do you want special stationery for invoices?

In order for a vendor to get it right, a visit may be necessary.

Choosing a vendor

6

Deciding on vendors to send your document to may be difficult if you do not know the market place well. Details of vendors can be sought from trade associations, *Yellow Pages* or trade and computer magazines. Ideally a choice should be made between firms which are:

- Leaders or specialists in your type of business in that they have some experience of selling and developing systems in your business area.
- Firms locally based, if possible. This makes it easier to get demonstrations and back-up support if needed.
- Firms with a good reputation and a sound background in computer sales and development.
- Firms with a sound financial base.
- Local business contacts known to you.

Waiting for replies

In your specification you may have set a deadline for receipt of replies. Once this deadline has passed you might have received a number of replies, but do not expect all vendors to reply.

If you send your specification details to (say) six vendors, then you will almost certainly hear from some of them before the cut-off date. If you hear nothing at all then you have probably sent an unrealistic set of specifications. It may now be worth your while chasing up a few vendors to find out their reaction. If your specifications are found to be unrealistic, then at least you have made the discovery before embarking on major investment and upheaval.

Making a comparison

If you have a number of vendor specifications to choose from, you will be able to compare the offerings and, what is more, question one vendor in respect of points brought up by another. In practice, some of the specifications may not fit your business and through a process of elimination you may arrive at a clear choice.

On the other hand, a choice may be less clear. The following guidelines may be useful when deciding on a vendor proposal:

1. *How closely does the proposal fit your specification?* The situation may well arise where not all proposals meet your exact requirements as written down. You should bear in mind that the experience of the vendor may be such that they have improved on your specification. You will have to make your own judgement on this.
2. *Does the system fall within your budget?* If a vendor has responded, then it is likely that the quotation will be within your budgetary figure. If the proposal meets your specification then the next step is to see whether the vendor is offering *value for money*. Absolute cost may not be the best criterion on which to base judgement.
3. *Does the proposal include after-sales support?* Support is very important in the early days of such a project. In practice a lot can go wrong. You need some assurance that you will get help if you get a system failure, a loss of data or any other unforeseen problem. Some proposals will come with guarantee of hardware and software maintenance for the first year or two years of a project together with telephone support if you have any queries.
4. *Does the proposal include installation and staff training?* However good you or your staff are at computer applications, some on-site help and training will always speed up the implementation process and help you to avoid problems. If you specified the need for on-site training, then make sure it is adequate for your needs.
5. *Are there any hidden costs?* Check on such costs as staff training, maintenance contracts and telephone support.

Again, such information should be contained in the vendor's proposals.

6. *Can they deliver on time?* This should include delivery, installation and staff training. If you are not sure whether installation includes software as well as hardware, then you should ask for clarification.

7. *Future development capabilities?* You should be aware of any future enhancements that may be possible with your system. Computer systems should grow and develop with the company. Most systems, however, tend to have a limit to the extent that they can be developed. You will need to be satisfied that the limitations of the system will not hinder progress in the future or incur heavy development costs. For example, how many computer stations can the system be expanded to; how much disk storage can the system support?

8. *How much change will the system impose on the business?* Although computer systems should be made to fit into the way a business runs and works, the implementation of a computerised system will, inevitably, impose changes in procedures. You should be aware of what changes are likely to occur and whether they are acceptable. For example, does the software require completely different stationery? Does the system mean that customer statements will be in a different format? Again, only you will be able to measure the degree of acceptability of these changes.

9. *What is the background and experience of the vendors?* There are a large number of 'cowboys' in the market who know no more about computing in business than you do; avoid them at whatever cost. If you are in doubt about the credentials of a vendor, then ask some direct questions about their background and experience in this line of business. Any vendor with a good background will volunteer this information without you asking for it.

10. *How do they want to be paid?* Whether cash on delivery or instalments or some other method, such information will, no doubt, prove important to you. When you receive details, much of it may be fairly technical in detail and require specialist knowledge in order to understand it. If this is the case, then you should refer back to the vendor for clarification.

It may well benefit you to see a demonstration of the proposed system before you commit yourself. This is commonly offered by vendors who may request that you make a visit. Such demonstrations are very useful if you need to clear up a few points.

If at this stage there is still doubt or confusion in your mind about what system to choose, employing consultancy help may well prove to be a wise move. If you do this, then it is worth inquiring of a consultant whether he or she has a vested interest in any particular supplier – it may influence the advice given to you. Also, some consultants may have a preference for a particular computer manufacturer or software firm. Consultancy fees may often appear to be high in the short run, but the long term implications of opting for a system that is not best for your business could prove far more expensive and even catastrophic.

One of the best ways of selecting a good consultant is by recommendation from a friend, colleague or trading association. Whatever method of choosing a consultant you use, it is still worth asking something about background and experience.

The next chapter is an attempt to put most of what has been covered so far into context, and as you read you should try to draw parallels with your own business circumstances.

7 A case study

The facts □ The problems □ The new system □ Getting
organised □ Getting started □ Developments □ Other
benefits □ System evaluation □ Computerising the sales
function □ Completing accounts □ Further development

This case study is based on a fictitious firm, NatWest Light Ltd,
that manufactures and markets domestic lighting equipment. The
range of equipment manufactured can be quite extensive, but the
mainstream activity involves the manufacture of thirty different
ranges of torches, ten different ranges of light fitting, ten types of
table lamps and a range of specialist lights often made to customer
order.

The company prides itself on its reputation for meeting orders
from retailers and overseas customers on time. Some simple facts
about the company may put it into some kind of perspective.

The facts

Number of employees:		
Production: Shop Floor		15
Production: Administration		2
Marketing, Sales and Distribution		5
Dispatch		4
Accounts		3
Managerial		4
	Total staff	34

Turnover	£12 million
Expected number of orders	400 per month
Number of suppliers	100
Number of regular customers	650
Average stock value on premises	£2.5 million
Number of different items held in stock	5,000

Although the above depicts the state of the company at present, this
represents a 50 per cent growth in the volume of trade since five
years ago, when the company was formed.

Projected turnover growth for the next five years is estimated at about 15 to 20 per cent per annum. With such growth, it is anticipated that more capital equipment will be required and there is likely to be a need to employ more production shop floor staff (probably two) and an extra person to cope with dispatch of goods. The company already has its production staff working on regular overtime and equipment working six days a week when production to meet orders needs to be high, hence the need for more staff and capital equipment.

The problems

All administrative procedures are done manually by clerical staff at present. Although the company sees no problem in coping with the extra capital equipment and staff, it anticipates a problem in information flows which cannot be overcome by simply employing more administration staff. In fact, information needs are not being properly satisfied by the current manual system. The company has identified the following information problems which will get worse with the projected growth:

---

1. Maintaining efficient stock levels becomes increasingly difficult. With the more essential stock items, such as differing types of flex (there are fifty in all), the company holds far more stock than is probably needed, because it cannot afford to run out. It is estimated that stock values are £500,000 higher than necessary, a figure that may well grow rapidly, with expansion.
2. Keeping track of customer orders is becoming a strain, endangering the reputation the firm has for being able to meet customer orders punctually.
3. At any one time, there are up to 100 purchase orders with a range of suppliers, some of whom are overseas. Keeping checks on suppliers is becoming difficult because the information on orders still outstanding is coming to the Production Manager too late. On more than one occasion, the manufacture of key products had to be held up because of shortages of certain components. The problem tends to be resolved by resorting to even higher stock levels of key components being held.
4. Information about customers owing money to the firm is not forthcoming at the right time. Quite often customer debt is left outstanding longer than it needs to be and customers exceed their credit limits because information does not come quickly enough. Of the average total of customer debt of £1.2 million, it

is estimated that this figure could be reduced to an average of
£800,000 without damaging company sales. Also, bad debts
could fall by half to about £50,000 per annum.

It is important to stress that the company is far from disaster, but
sees that if something is not done about these potential problems
over the next two years, a serious problem could evolve.

The new system

The decision to computerise was taken as a result of a visit by a
computer consultant, who advised that the company should acquire
the following:

- A multi-user computer with four terminals. The computer
  would have a 110 megabyte hard disk where the main files
  would go. The system would operate with the Xenix
  operating system software.
- A range of application packages including integrated
  accounts, stock control and spreadsheet all being available
  for multi-user access.

The strategy was to computerise the stock control function first,
as this was identified as the main problem area. A decision could
have been made to implement *all* applications simultaneously, but
this was felt to be too ambitious. One thing at a time was regarded
as the best policy.

When the equipment was installed, one terminal was positioned
in the Production Manager's office, one in stores and two with the
Production Administration staff. The file server was also positioned
in the Production office where the two Production Administration
staff were located. The consultant who organised the installation
also arranged two days' on-site training for the two Production
Administration staff, the person in charge of stores and the
Production Manager. The two-day training was focused on setting
up and running stock control and purchase order systems.

Getting organised

The next stage was to place all stock information onto the stock control system. This process took the following form:

1. The person in charge of stores had to ensure that *all* stock
   cards were up to date in terms of having one stock card for
   each item of stock; the description for each item was correct,
   cost prices were accurate and location where stock could be
   found was correct.

   During this exercise, some errors were found and corrected
   with improvements being made.

   The company always kept on stock record cards an estimated
   lead time for ordering stock quantities, reorder quantities,
   usual supplier and stock movement histories.
2. The production team, who were to be responsible for
   maintaining the stock control system, had decided to scan the
   stock records carefully, allocating new codes for their stock
   items. It was felt that this was long overdue and now was the
   best time to implement the system. Essentially, the stock codes
   that were already in existence would still be used but each code
   would be prefixed with either A, B, C or Z to indicate the
   classification of stock. Basically, classification 'A' meant the
   stock was expensive and should be held only when needed in
   the short term. At the other end of the spectrum, 'Z' indicated
   very little cost involved in both buying and holding stock. The
   purpose of this was to get stock lists in the order they were
   required, a technique they learnt during training. Also, the
   stock code would have a three digit code following the
   classification code to indicate where in the warehouse the
   stock would be located. Again, this produces a listing of stock
   that would prove useful for stores management, producing
   'picking lists' and checking on stock quickly.
3. When everything was complete and, as a result, the data was
   ready for input, the decision was made to create all the stock
   records on computer during the weekend. By the weekend
   chosen the manual stock records were ready; there was always
   the fear that if this process were delayed for any time, the
   figures would soon be out of date. A Saturday was chosen, with
   four operators working through the day on the terminals, to get
   the information onto the computer. Two of the staff needed a
   little training, but by the end of the day all records were entered
   on the computer.

At this point, the only thing missing on the stock records was
the actual stock level. This was intentionally left until last, because
of the problem that a time delay in getting any information on to

the computer would render all stock levels useless. Before progressing further, a printout of the stock details entered was extracted and a few alterations were made, as well as three records being added which had been omitted originally.

Another visit from their consultant led to the advice that all such records should be backed up before continuing. A tape drive was purchased and installed onto the system where files would be backed up. A simple procedure was designed to allow this. It was also agreed that such a backing-up procedure would be carried out, as of habit, at the end of each day. A simple program routine was written on the computer to do all the necessary work; all the operator had to do was to run this program.

Getting started

The next stage was to enter all stock quantities and implement the system. It was decided to do this on the following Friday and Saturday. During these two days, stock levels were taken and stock quantities (opening stock balances) were adjusted to reflect actual stocks in the warehouse.

The responsibility for keeping stock levels up to date was that of the person in charge of the stock. As from the Monday, every issue or receipt of stock was to be entered as a stock movement. This implementation went extremely smoothly, and without too much disruption to the normal business. The company went on using the system almost unhindered for a month. It became apparent to the Production Manager that the ability to sit at a computer and inquire about stock quantities at any time was an invaluable tool for his job, especially when planning production. Also, it was found that the low-stock reports were extremely useful when planning what orders to place with suppliers.

Only one problem occurred when, as a result of error, the stock files were corrupted. This happened at 10.45 one morning. The Production Manager telephoned the consultant and was soon able to put things right by restoring the stock details from the previous day (which had been backed up onto the tape) and re-entering the morning's movement figures. The whole process wasted just two hours, soon to be recovered during the process of the day's work.

At the end of the month, another stock-take exercise was made to see how closely it matched the computer data. The differences were small and minor and easily corrected, and new procedures for the collection and input of data were quickly drawn up.

Developments

During the month, the Production Administration staff were sent on a computer appreciation course for two days. As a result of this, they requested the facility of a word processing package for their terminals to replace the need for a typewriter. The Production Manager, commending them for their insight and enthusiasm, promptly purchased two single-user versions of Wordstar Professional Version 5 for their terminals. Within one week, both staff were using their packages in preference to their typewriters. In addition to this, they learnt the technique of linking the reports generated by the stock control system to the word processor. In other words, they learnt to get the stock control reports to write to a file on their disks, and were then able to use the word processing package to incorporate the stock control output into reports and letters to produce a more professional standard of report.

One of the obvious problems with the computerised stock system was the fact that low stocks could not automatically generate an order for new stocks because the computer did not take into consideration what was already on order. In fact on more than one occasion an order was placed in error with a supplier for new stock which had already been ordered. It was felt, therefore, that the next stage was to implement a Purchase Order System (POS). This application would be integrated with stock control in that, when an order was placed for stock, a stock record field called 'on order' would record the amount on order. When the goods were eventually received, the stock record would be updated by reducing the amount on order and increasing the amount in stock. The system would print purchase orders. It would also keep a record of all outstanding purchase orders, enabling the company to chase up orders that were late.

The first step for the purchase order system was to decide on the pre-printed stationery to be used. The existing stationery for generating order forms was used and a local stationer was commissioned to produce the forms as continuous stationery.

When the stationery arrived, the purchase order system was set up and, after a lot of trial and error, the printing of orders matched the stationery. One of the Production Administration staff quickly placed all outstanding orders onto the system and found that printing orders to suppliers using this system was relatively quick and easy and a substantial improvement on typing orders and having to file them away. With telephone orders, staff were still able to enter purchase details without necessarily having to print a purchase order.

Other benefits

Almost immediately, the implementation of the purchase order system enhanced the stock control system and made it easier to see any outstanding orders that had not been received after the dates expected. Also, the ordering of more stock when stock reached reorder levels was much more effective. Within a few weeks of the system running, and responsible staff becoming more capable and confident with the system, stocks held on the premises could be reduced as a need to hold large stock levels was less apparent.

One of the other benefits to be derived from the computerisation of both stock recording and purchase ordering was that staff had more time to study the supply of stock from suppliers and 'shop around' the market place for better purchases. Also, the business having a sharper awareness of which suppliers were delivering on time had the effect of making suppliers more responsive to expected delivery dates.

In all it was estimated that the value of stock in hand fell by £200,000 (saving an estimated £13,000 a year in holding costs), and about another £10,000 would be saved in a year because of the chance to switch to better suppliers.

7

System evaluation

The company board, at an evaluation meeting, had come to the conclusion that the computerisation project was a resounding success and should be extended into accounts. The Accounts Manager, therefore, was given the job of investigating the feasibility of computerising sales, invoicing and sales order processing functions of the business. This was largely a result of the Production Manager complaining that the effectiveness of stock control was hindered due to the fact that it was not clear from the computer what stocks were earmarked for sale. If it was clear what stocks were allocated for sale, it would be easier to decide accurately what needed reordering and, more important, more rational decisions could be made regarding production planning; too much time was still being wasted switching production schedules at the last minute in order to meet pressing orders. Meanwhile, the Production Manager was given the go-ahead to implement bill of materials as a way of enhancing the stock control system.

Computerising the sales function

The Accounts Manager began by using the same consultant to help decide a strategy for computerising sales. The first stage involved acquiring three extra terminals and upgrading the system to allow these additional terminals to be linked to it. Additional printers were also acquired. One terminal was installed in the Accounts Manager's office, one in the main accounts office and one with the sales clerk.

As soon as the system was upgraded and the additional hardware installed, four members of staff, one of whom was the Accounts Manager, were trained to use the computer for sales ledger and invoicing by a trainer who came to the firm and trained the staff on site. The training lasted two days.

In addition to the sales ledger and invoicing routines, sales order processing enabled the company to process orders when they arrived from the customer in a very functional way. If the goods could be dispatched immediately, the details would be used to update the stock records to indicate that there was an outstanding sales order pending which would use these goods; the details would then be entered to an outstanding sales order file. The outstanding sales order details could then be used by accounts to ensure customers were receiving their orders on time, and could be used by production to help plan production schedules.

From here, the four staff formed a small committee, chaired by the Accounts Manager, to decide on a plan of action. The plan decided upon took the following form:

---

1. Design and order special continuous stationery for both the invoices and sales acknowledgement forms.
2. Set up and tailor the sales ledger, sales order processing (SOP) and invoicing systems.
3. Collect details of *all* customers and enter this information to the sales ledger, placing an adjustment into each account to indicate how much is owed by each customer.
4. Enter every invoice, credit note, debit note and all accounts adjustment details to the sales ledger until ready to implement the invoicing system.
5. Enter details of all those sales orders that have not yet been met by the firm, thereby updating the stock records so that the production section can see what is on order by looking at the stock records.

The first four stages were implemented smoothly, although staff did not appreciate the benefits of entering such details other than being able to print customer statements of account. This system was left to run one month before extending it. Meanwhile, the following preparations were being made:

- Each stock record was being prepared with an analysis code, unit price, unit description and VAT code. The purpose of this was to integrate invoicing with stock control. When an invoice was raised, the stock details could be used to make invoice production easier, and to update the stock records with the issues of stock the invoices would represent.
- The method chosen was also designed to allow future sales analysis to indicate categories of lights to be grouped. For example, all table lamps were prefixed with T. Each stock item had attached to it a VAT code.
- In addition to linking invoicing with stock control, the company wanted to integrate them with the sales ledger fully. In other words when the invoice is raised, the sales ledger is automatically updated.

This was all done in conjunction with operating the sales ledger by itself for one month. In the second month, the next stage could go ahead.

As each customer was about to be invoiced or sent a credit note, the operator would use the invoicing function to achieve it. This went ahead with remarkable fruition. It meant that the stock file was now being updated with an issue almost immediately the transaction had occurred. In addition to this, the whole process of invoicing had been speeded up. The operators soon got into the habit of processing such transactions as a batch processing run at 11.00 a.m. each weekday.

The information being supplied to both the accounts and marketing personnel proved invaluable. In fact, for the first time, the Marketing department could now analyse sales performance almost as soon as it happened.

In addition to this, keeping a check on customer credit limits more effectively meant fewer customers were being allowed to go over their credit limit without proper authorisation.

Within one month of this, sales order processing was fully implemented. This proved easy because most of the preparation had been done. As a starting point, all outstanding orders were placed on file and then all orders received from customers were processed through the computerised sales order processing system. Operators soon recognised the benefits and found themselves with more time to concentrate on customer relations and promoting their products.

In addition to many of the accounting functions being met, those responsible for maintaining stock levels not only knew what was in stock at any time, but also what was on order and what stock had been allocated to sales.

Completing accounts

After six months of computerisation, a number of minor errors had been ironed out and the company was running the system with a good deal of success.

The next stage in the development of the system was to extend the role of computerised accounts to include both the nominal ledger and purchase ledger.

Starting with the nominal ledger, the company soon had this function set up and integrated with the rest of the operation. All journal entries were, at first, carried out by the Accounts Manager. Incorporated with the nominal ledger was the cash book which was used by one of the accounts staff to enter all cash transactions. One of the early benefits on computerising this function was improved control of cash movements.

During this development, bill of materials had also become well established within the computerised system. The Production Department was responsible for this and it allowed them to define their finished products as a collection of components. The bill of materials proved useful to accounts in measuring the amount of work in progress. The main benefit to production was being able to see what the company could produce of any product with what was in stock. It also speeded up the purchasing quite considerably by being able to list all extra stock needed in order to meet given production schedules.

Future development

After eighteen months the company had seen its information systems develop a long way. One of the main future developments will be to extend the size of the system to allow more users to have access to the information on the system. The marketing personnel's information requirements are such that they need a good deal of information on sales. A terminal was installed in their office to facilitate this requirement.

Over time, as the system developed, the company organised itself quite effectively in order to get data onto the computer as quickly as possible, with as little fuss as possible.

The major problem caused as a result of computerisation is that the company now finds it much more difficult to recruit staff of the right calibre, even when it has increased its staff salaries to reflect the additional skills required to perform the tasks.

At present, the company has computer expertise among its managers who have a number of developments they wish to get under way, payroll almost certainly being the next project. It is anticipated that the information processing over the next few years will go on changing.

The latest evaluation report showed that the company was meeting its information needs well and would be able to cope with future expansion easily.

7

8   More on costs of computerising

What you pay for □ Paying for it all □ Taxation benefits □
Rental □ Loan of a machine

What you pay for

Business people tend to focus almost entirely on the initial cost of
the hardware of the computer system. Generally this interest is
stimulated by advertisements in magazines and Sunday supplements.
However, the alluring packages paraded in such places are more
in keeping with image building. They sometimes lead to impulse
buying with expensive results. They are unlikely to suit the needs
of the majority of businesses. And it is the needs of the business
that should be considered with great care long before the hardware
or the software is evaluated. It is unwise in the extreme to look only
at the initial cost of the equipment, which might turn out to be
virtually useless when installed.

Paying for applications software

In general, the price of software reflects its effectiveness and
popularity. Every business needs effective communications and
accurate accounting methods. Translated into computer terms, this
means a word processor and an accounting package. Since both
of these activities are so common, there is a multitude of programs
to choose from. Some are simplified almost to a point where they
hardly take any advantage of the power of the computer while
others use almost every feature of the machinery. Some will be
self-contained while others will be integrated with other packages.
Some will be designed for use on only one computer while others
will be fully prepared for network or multi-user operation. Some
are very cheap, others very expensive for what they do. There will
be a selection of programs that are designed for just your type
of business.

Suppliers will need to have some idea of your budget to help you

properly. Good suppliers will also spend some considerable time
finding out from you what it is you want your computer to do. They
will try to find out the level of sophistication you are expecting and
will try to match it with the appropriate programs. There will be
an element of chance, because there are so many programs and also
because different suppliers will be familiar with different programs.
The supplier will be thinking of you as a future reference site, and
will not suggest a cheap program if it is going to be inadequate for
your needs. Conversely, you may not need the extensive features
of a high price program and no supplier wants to be branded as
too expensive.

Your choice of software will influence the choice of hardware.
Some programs simply will not run on some computers and so the
choice of software limits your choice of hardware. (The converse
is also true.) The cost of computer hardware is gradually falling.
When the power of the machines is taken into account, this fall
is quite rapid. Whatever hardware you purchase, you can expect
it to be out of date within a year or two and it will not fetch much
on the second-hand market. This means that, although it may
continue to do its job perfectly well for many years, there comes
a time when greater power and sophistication will be needed for
a growing business. Generally speaking, it is not economical to
update hardware. Software, however, can often be updated easily
and many software houses have a policy of including upgrades within
their software maintenance contracts.

Paying for hardware

Hardware costs are perhaps the easiest to quantify. If you have a
clear idea of the specification of machine you require, then you can
look in magazines and find out the price you will have to pay. You
will find that within each category of machine there will be a range
of two-to-one depending upon where you shop, what make of
machine you are looking at, whether or not the cost of the monitor,
keyboard and operating system is included, what after-sales service
is on offer. It is reasonable to ask your suppliers about discounts,
but it is very often self-defeating to press them too hard. When you
start to haggle, the first thing that you will lose out on is the quality
of after-sales service. If everyone cuts into suppliers' margins, then
they cannot afford to employ the better quality staff and your support
begins to suffer. Don't haggle about the cost of any particular item
as the smart supplier will recoup at least some of the loss on a less
tangible item. If you take all your business to one supplier, then

you will be seen to be a valued customer and can expect discounts of 10 per cent or so.

Paying for peripherals

The cost of your computer can pale into insignificance if you require high quality peripherals. Printers, plotters, scanners, modems, large monitors, etc., can all exceed the cost of the computer itself. A desk top publishing installation may cost £8,000 and be driven by a £2,000 computer.

Paying for software

When you start to put the system together, you will think of ever more tasks for it to perform. As you do so, you will be clocking up additional software costs. Each time you want the system to do something more, you will need a program to instruct the computer how to do it. For instance, basic printing programs (routines) are included with all operating systems, but if you want your laser printer to do fancy printing, then you will probably need special software to do the job. Adding a modem immediately calls for a communications program. In most cases the software for special peripherals is sold separately from the peripheral itself and incurs the purchaser in additional cost.

Paying for cabling

Cables to connect parts of a system together are costed separately from the parts themselves and may quickly eat up £100 or more. Cabling for a network system will be a more formal consideration, but £10 per terminal would be a typical materials cost. Labour costs for drilling through walls and dressing the cable neatly and safely around the building is quite likely to double or treble that figure. Doing it yourself just takes you away from your business and you have no recourse if it doesn't work.

Paying for delivery and installation

However delivery is effected, there will be costs. Collecting the gear yourself will take you away from your own (profitable?) work. Delivery by supplier will impose a cost somewhere else which will have to be passed on to you either directly or indirectly. The same applies to installation, both of the software onto the machines and of the hardware into your premises.

There are considerable benefits to be gained from paying reasonable charges for both of these jobs. Regarding delivery, if you decide to collect the machinery and then walk out of your supplier's door and drop it, you will have to sort out the insurance, you will have to buy another machine, you will have to wait a bit longer to get your system up and running. Regarding installation, you would not be reading this book if you were able to do the job as well as a competent supplier. If you do not get the installation right your system will not work as well as it could. If you run into difficulties then you will have to pay for call-out charges as your supplier isn't going to be happy fielding telephone calls from you if you are seen to be doing things 'on the cheap'. As in all walks of life, expertise is worth paying for.

All this presupposes that you have chosen your suppliers well and have not been conned by a bunch of cowboys. It will pay great dividends to develop good relationships with competent suppliers. You should not insult them by trying to get something for nothing, but it is reasonable for you to ask them to justify their charges. When you are supplied with a breakdown of their charges you may find that there are things that you can have done more cheaply, which in turn will save them time and save you more money. When the system is delivered, installed and shown to be working, pay up reasonably promptly. By failing to do so you may find yourself neglected because the supplier's response could well be: 'Bloggs & Co.? Let them wait. . . . They kept us waiting six weeks for our money.'

Buy a working system rather than a machine and some software because there are numerous pitfalls which can trap the novice trying to install software on a machine. It is still the exception for a manual to explain all the details of an installation procedure clearly enough for inexperienced users. Your supplier may very well make no charge for installing one or two pieces of software for you. At the same time good suppliers will also add features to your system which will make it very much easier to use. If your system is to be a network, for instance, then there is really no alternative to having the software set up completely by the suppliers. You will have recourse to them if they do not get it right and the onus is on them to get it working in the first place. It may well be that problems will be encountered during installation and the resulting cost will then have to be borne by the suppliers. Moreover, you are unlikely to be charged the full labour cost because the technicians will be able to deal with emergencies for other customers at the same time as setting up your system.

By having the system installed into your premises by your suppliers, you can ensure that problems that arise will be appreciated quickly and taken care of with the minimum of fuss. Also the technicians might well spot problems with the location of the equipment and advise that it be placed in a better position. They will also be able to advise on the environment. Your staff will be able to get free advice concerning the care and operation of the system as there are few technicians who are not willing to demonstrate their knowledge and skill with the computer equipment. If your supplier is a relatively small, local firm, then friendly relations should be developed over this period which will pay dividends when you make stupid mistakes or other things go wrong. And you should always expect things to go wrong. The trick is to make sure that you can recover with minimum cost to the business when they do.

Paying for insurance

You turn up one morning at your office to find that it is surrounded by fire engines and police. There has been a gas explosion in the building nextdoor and your offices have been gutted by fire. Nothing can be salvaged. How long will it take you to restart your business? Have you lost most of the information on which your business relies? Can you afford to do so? Do you break down, bewail your luck and file for bankruptcy or do you call your insurance broker, take over offices in the next street, replenish your stock, load your programs and data from your back-ups onto your new computer and set to work? A quotation from the report of the Official Receiver may serve to highlight the importance of adequate insurance cover.

The director had anticipated that the company would begin to trade profitably in the second year, but in May 1988 a leak occurred in the flat above the company's offices, which flooded the computers, damaged the hardware and wiped out the database information. Unfortunately the insurance lapsed on 1st January 1988 and since the company was under-capitalised it was unable to recover from the disaster.

Paying for hardware maintenance

From time to time you have to change the battery on your car. The chances are that you may have to do the same with your computer system because the internal time-of-day clock is maintained by a small battery when the power is switched off. You occasionally have more serious problems with your car and the same will be true of your computer system. Disk drives fail, power supplies break down, keyboards and switches jam, circuit boards develop faults, printers refuse to work, visual displays distort, cables break. If you have someone on your staff who can deal with the multitude of simple problems that can occur *and* if you can suffer a day or two's delay without jeopardising your business, then you can get along successfully without a maintenance contract of some kind. Otherwise, you should ensure that you have either a maintenance contract or a special insurance agreement in force at all times.

If you have no maintenance agreement, you can call on your supplier for assistance or you can engage a specialist maintenance company. Both will resent trying to help you over the phone – you will be trying to use their resources without paying – and so they will simply get you to agree to have an engineer attend your site. Without a contract, you will probably have to wait a day or two and the cost of the whole operation will be charged to you. If it turns out to be a plug that is not making contact properly, you could end up paying several hundred pounds simply to have the plug pushed in. If a hard disk goes down then the bill could be a thousand pounds or more. The engineer will provide you with a report on the fault and the repair work that has been done. There may be other things that need attention, and a good engineer would probably advise you what should be done. Provided the engineer gets your system working again for you, then the maintenance company has fulfilled its obligation to you and you will have to pay the bill even if your computer system stops working a day or so later. Unless you are well versed in electronics and computer systems, you will not be able to judge the quality of work or the overall health of your machines.

A standard maintenance agreement, costing between 10 and 15 per cent of the hardware price per annum, shifts the burden of assessing the needs of your system to the maintenance company. It will be in their interests to keep your machines working properly and it is they who will have to foot the bill for that new hard disk. You will not be free from problems, but you will be relieved of the burden of getting them resolved.

Maintenance agreements can be arranged to suit your needs. Large companies often contract for on-site engineers for immediate response. Short response times will be very expensive because the maintenance company will need to employ more engineers. A common contract in small business is for an eight-hour response. This means that an engineer will be on site the following day. It

does not mean that your computer will be working the next day.
If your business cannot tolerate more than a day or so delay
then you can arrange for extra facilities to be provided. The
best way to do this is to identify the critical activities in your
business when you are specifying your system and determine the
minimum configuration that will support them. Then you can,
perhaps with the help of your supplier, plan a system that will
enable you to keep going even if part of the system is faulty.
Or you can contract for loan machines to be provided if the
repair is going to take too long. There will be a cost penalty
for either approach.

Paying for software maintenance

Software maintenance will only be required for specialist programs
or those critical for the wellbeing of the business. In such cases,
however, they are mandatory. Suppliers will resent you telephoning
them day after day with questions about the operation of the software
unless you pay for the service.

The plain fact is that from time to time things do go wrong with
computer files. People switch off machines without exiting from the
programs properly. The network may be shut down without all
terminals having logged off. There may be interruptions to the mains
power supply for various reasons. Temperature, humidity, thunder-
storms, 'dirty' mains power, and many other things can adversely
affect computer systems. In general the effects are unpredictable
and you will need real help.

The annual cost of software maintenance will generally be about
15 per cent of the initial cost of the package. This will probably
entitle you to updates to the system as they become available together
with access to expert assistance when things go wrong. The present
trend is for software houses to provide assistance by modem. With
this method, the programmers can take control of your machine
over the telephone and determine the problems directly. They can
correct faults and update programs at the same time. Your staff
will need to ensure that the various pieces of equipment are turned
on and properly connected, but they will not need to know how
to operate them. However, if you do have a modem and
communications software as part of your system you may find them
useful in your business activities. You would have access to Prestel
and specialist databases anywhere in the world. You would, however,
accrue telephone charges and connection charges for use of such
facilities.

Paying for training

There will be cost associated with training. It could be a direct and visible cost which appears on an invoice from the training company or the cost of sending employees to courses at the local technical college or adult education centre. In the second case some indirect costs will begin to appear. If the course is held during working hours the employees' work will still need to be done. Training will help employees to be more effective much sooner. They would probably see you as a 'good' employer and would be more receptive to the notion that the business takes an interest in its employees' welfare, thus boosting confidence and, possibly, loyalty. On the other side of the coin is the fact that a well trained employee can command a higher wage and is also much more mobile, so you could end up losing your entire investment to a competitor.

Without training, costs mount up and can even threaten the success of the computerisation project. You will be paying your employees while they are trying to get to grips with the system. Their productivity will suffer. They will feel and sometimes voice negative emotions regarding the management of the business. ('My boss expects me to do my job *and* to learn all about the computer'.) More seriously, the majority will not explore the possibilities that exist within the computer system. They are likely to end up doing things inefficiently, having an incomplete idea of the capabilities of the system and even getting things wrong. Methods of working may be adopted that will eventually lead to a breakdown of the system.

Training costs should be budgeted for with the idea of the employee learning good working practices and becoming more productive quickly and thus repaying the initial outlay in a very short period of time. The best plan, which will reap the greatest benefit in the long term, is to commit employees to learning as much as possible about the system at the time it is delivered and installed. As soon as it is working properly, employees should be trained on all aspects of the software that is specific to their work. If, at the same time as the transfer of skills takes place, the employees also gain an *understanding* of the reasons for various actions then they will be all the more valuable to the business and the returns on the training will be substantial.

Paying for consumables

The cost of disks, tapes, ribbons, toner cartridges, paper and other consumables can be considerable. It is only by controlling working practices that significant savings can be attained in this field. You cannot compromise on the disks and/or tapes without putting the security of your system at risk. Print quality can be affected if you skimp on printing materials, with an adverse effect on your company's image. It is best to shop around and compare prices for *identical* materials and to buy locally to cut down on delivery charges.

Paying for consultancy

You can waste a great deal of time trying to come to a decision about the machine you should buy, about the software you should buy, about the activities you should computerise. The computer market place is bewildering and unless you have a great deal of current experience the chances are that you need to engage someone to help you. If you are spending much less than £30,000 then you may find that employing a consultant for the whole project would be too expensive. However, you would probably be able to afford the services of a consultant for, say, a day or two to help you decide upon the areas within your business that are worth computerising and, at a later stage, to help you decide between systems that you have been offered.

If you belong to a professional organisation or trade association, then your first port of call in search of a consultant should be with them. Some consultants work very closely with particular dealers and may not be as independent as they would like you to believe. You will find that many consultants belong to professional organisations of their own, such as the Association of Professional Computer Consultants, which will give you some degree of confidence in their work and independence.

Paying for preparation and entry of initial data

With almost all applications, the computer system will require loading with some initial body of data. This could consist of mailing lists, accounting and stock control information, payroll details, production schedules, sales prospects, etc. The computer system will impose a discipline on the way the data has to be entered and this, in turn, will almost certainly require that you prepare the data to make the job easier to perform. Without this preparation the chance of errors is greatly increased. Because this work takes people away from the more productive tasks, there will be a cost penalty. Temporary help will be fairly easy to cost, but time and effort will still be required of existing employees.

Paying for breakdowns

It is certain that failures of some kind will occur from time to time. You may be able, with great effort and cost, to ensure that everything is fully controlled within your system. You can purchase fault-tolerant software that can keep going when something goes wrong with a piece of hardware. You can purchase a diesel generator that will take over immediately in the event of mains power failure. You can spend an awful lot of money to keep the system going in the event of disaster. But if you really warrant such a system, you should get specific advice on products and systems appropriate to your application. The problem is one of technology and is beyond the scope of this book.

Instead of trying to keep everything working it is better to accept that disaster is going to strike a few times a year. You then prepare for the inevitable and make sure that you can start up again with a minimum of fuss and expense.

One discipline that must be instilled into the staff is the concept of back-ups – i.e. copies, in machine-readable form, of everything on the computer. This usually means that copies are made on floppy disks or tape of the files that are stored on the hard disk(s). These procedures can be refined to disperse responsibility and to take care of departmental errors or failures.

In the simplest case, where a small, stand alone computer system is installed, the individuals making use of the system should make back-ups at the end of each session during which they have entered anything new or altered existing details. Only those files that have been altered need to be backed up – not everything on the machine. The software developers will normally indicate what needs to be backed up whenever the programs have been used. Your supplier may well set up command files that simplify the job.

Paying for it all

A new business is invariably short of cash and a going concern usually needs as much working capital as possible. It is therefore unwise to tie up money in an asset such as a computer which has no obvious earning power for most businesses. A computer is a dubious asset because it depreciates quickly, the used computer market is awash with machines, the market is still changing rapidly, and the software that you need to make the computer function has very little resale value. Paying for software is like having to pay in one go for all the petrol you are going to use in your car for the next five years. The only way to overcome the frightening prospect of instant depreciation is to make the machine work very hard, to save you time, to save you accountancy fees, to watch over your stock and to derive useful management information with which to control your business.

Cash

There is little incentive to pay cash for computer equipment unless you happen to find exactly what you need at a drastically reduced price, say by at least 30 or 40 per cent. Such a reduction is only likely to be found at a closing-down sale and then it is likely to be end-of-line stock that is difficult to sell. You might be lucky buying second hand, perhaps at an auction. Success here depends upon a thorough knowledge of what you need and the skill to ascertain the quality of the equipment to be purchased. Purchasing this way is fraught with danger, but could be of value if you were enhancing an existing network or looking for an extra machine to provide back-up facilities or spare parts. Regular suppliers are likely to shun you if you go to them hoping that they will help you with your prize. Expect to pay full rates for exploratory examinations and for maintenance. If you buy cheap then it is likely that you will find that you have end-of-line machines or machines that have limitations that are not at first obvious. Find out the specifications of the equipment *before* you buy.

Overdraft

If you have overdraft facilities, then the marginal cost of financing a small computer system this way would probably be less than any other method. Perhaps it is too painless in that the implication of the loss of working capital may not become apparent until too late. If you consider taking this route, it would be a good idea to discuss it with your bank manager before any deals are struck with the computer supplier. After all, the computer hardware will have a certain amount of value as an asset and you might be able to increase your borrowing facility.

Loan

A loan from a bank or other institution will probably cost a little more than you would pay on your overdraft, but it has some advantages. First of all, it does not immediately reduce your working capital. Second, you have a clear statement of the repayment schedule and you can see what effect these costs are going to have on your cash-flow for the duration of the loan. Third, there is a definite end to the repayments. Again a discussion with your bank manager about a business loan can only be helpful.

Government schemes

You will have investigated all the government supported schemes as a matter of course while setting up your business. Computer systems can be financed through a business development loan scheme.

Lease

This method of financing will generally be more expensive than directly through a bank. Unless you are in a business that can command preferential rates (an established solicitor's practice, for instance), then you will pay more because of the increased risks that the leasing company is willing to undertake. Indeed, it will have to find a buyer for your old computer system if your business fails and, as mentioned above, second-hand computer systems do not fetch much money.

Once you have proved your credit worthiness by paying regularly for a year or so, you will find it easier to extend your lease when you require more machines or a better computing system. Simply by topping up your lease, you can finance your second machine or replace your network with a newer, faster one.

Another aspect of leasing that makes it more attractive is the fact that you are entitled to claim full tax relief on every payment. Add to this the availability of additional working capital in the early stages and the prospect of committing your business to long term debt is less daunting.

Taxation benefits

The following example is aimed at stimulating thought about the ways you can finance your system and how much such methods may, or may not, benefit your business.

£10,000 lease

For each tax year of the rental, 100 per cent of the rental amount can be claimed against tax.

If we take a typical rate of £80 per thousand per quarter we get a payment of £800 per quarter or £3,200 per year.

Year	Allowance £	Tax saving £
1	3,200	800
2	3,200	800
3	3,200	800
4	3,200	800
5	3,200	800
Total over 5 years		£4,000
Total payments		£16,000
Net payments		£12,000

The benefit of an additional £10,000 working capital being available to the company can make leasing very attractive.

£10,000 purchase

A purchase entitles you to claim 25 per cent per year of the capital amount against tax on a reducing basis. Writing down allowance of 25 per cent:

Year	Allowance £	Tax saving £
1	2,500	625
2	1,875	469
3	1,406	352
4	1,054	264
5	791	198
Total over 5 years		£1,908

A large cash outlay will mean either a loss of earnings on the money or, more likely, the need to borrow. In either case there is a financial penalty which will make outright purchase far less attractive than it might appear at first sight.

Briefly, leasing is a very effective method of acquiring modern equipment with no capital outlay. All payments are tax-deductible. It is a hedge against inflation in that, at the end of the lease, you are paying with devalued money. Finally, and very importantly, it preserves existing credit lines and initial working capital. If you have faith in yourself and your business and need all your working capital as well as a computer, the fact that, with present tax rates, leasing costs a little more in the long run should not cause you concern.

Rental

It is possible to rent a computer, but it is an option that is not realistic except for short-term crises. A number of factors must be borne in mind. Long-term rental premiums are not commonly listed by the suppliers and you will probably have to negotiate for an acceptable rate. The supplier will have to bear the costs of maintenance and repair (depending upon the contract required), so the rates will have to reflect these costs and will certainly be more expensive than direct purchase or lease. Moreover, a long term contract may justifiably include penalty clauses for early termination. In addition to these limitations, it is unlikely that you will be able to find a supplier who would be willing to supply a *system* complete with software. Unless great care is taken as machines are returned or taken away for repair, you would be at greater risk of allowing valuable, sensitive or proprietory information to fall into the hands of unknown third parties.

Loan of a machine

A sole proprietor or a member of a small partnership could consider buying the computer system personally. The cost would probably be less than that of the family car. The business would then pay for the use of the machine and offset the loan payments paid by the individual. In this way the risk is shifted from the business to the individual. The equipment does not become an asset of the business and would not be subject to seizure upon liquidation. The individual would still own the computer system, but would have to find the remaining payments out of his or her own pocket.

When to acquire a computer

It is perhaps unwise to commit a new business to a computer system unless you can guarantee that it will be viable for at least a year. This means that you should have sufficient personal funds to enable you to live for a year without taking anything from your business, and your business should have funding to ensure its survival for a year even under adverse conditions. If the volume of business is going to be fairly small and the administration can be handled manually without putting a strain on anyone, then postpone the purchase of a computer until you really need one.

A growing business will be able to justify a system when the existing staff find the work load too much to complete within a normal working day. The cost of a computer will probably be less than that of employing a new member of staff. This would certainly be true in the long term because the running costs of a computer are very low and the computer can be used to speed up the non-productive tasks and release staff for more profitable activities. To remain competitive, and to have access to management information before it is out of date, the business will find that it cannot do without a computer when it has grown to an extent that routine administration tasks are removing staff from productive tasks.

Installing and running a computer system

This part deals with getting the system installed and running in a business. It includes practical aspects of installation including, for example, location and environment, as well as training operators and other staff.

It also discusses how best to change over from the methods and procedures currently in use to the new computerised methods.

Part 3 ends with a case study examining some of the problems that can occur if implementation is not well thought out and planned, especially when a business and its staff are not adequately prepared.

9 Practical aspects of installing a computer

Keeping the computer happy □ Keeping the user happy

This chapter provides you with guidelines which will help you to ensure that your computer is installed and working in minimum time and with a minimum amount of fuss and annoying problems.

Keeping the computer happy

Temperature is one important factor that must be taken into consideration when deciding where the computer will be placed. Hot, sunny positions, nearby radiators or fan heaters can lead to the machine becoming overheated. On the other hand, early winter mornings in offices where the heating is turned off overnight can lead to lubricants on components in disk drives and printers becoming too stiff to operate properly. Cold equipment is also more susceptible to condensation.

Temperature

Most electronic equipment works best at the temperature of a normal office, that is, around 20 °C (70 °F). If it is comfortable for humans, then it will be OK for computers. Wide departures from this value will invariably lead to malfunction which can be either (1) insidious, hidden, with the system apparently working normally or (2) catastrophic with total hardware failure with, perhaps, disk drives not starting, components breaking down and sometimes even smoke!
Failures that can be traced to excessively high or low temperatures might be beyond the scope of your maintenance contract and could result in a bill approaching half the original cost of the damaged equipment.

Heat can build up inside the computer even though the room temperature is not excessive. Wherever the ventilation slots are located and however well the designers have protected the fan and provided for hot air to be expelled, with enough ingenuity it will always be possible for the inventive user to thwart the design, stifle the ventilation and get the machine to malfunction. Papers, clothing, furniture, etc., can block the flow of air and even stop the fan from rotating.

Humidity

Humidity, both very high and very low, can have serious consequences for the reliability of computers. Moisture will condense out of the air in a hot, muggy room onto the cold surfaces of a machine or box of floppy disks brought in from, say, the cold boot of a car in winter. Such moisture can cause havoc while it persists inside a computer. Under these conditions, switching on the computer before it has warmed up can lead to major problems because the moist air will be sucked into the works by the fan. (An extreme example of such a situation occurred one cold January morning when a technician switched on the computer soon after the cleaner had washed the tiled floor. As the floor dried, the moisture-laden air was blown across the cold hard disk where it condensed causing a 'head-crash' which cost £2,000 to repair. It must be said, however, that moisture is unlikely to penetrate so easily to the surface of modern sealed Winchester type disks.)

At the other extreme of very low humidity, which occurs in centrally heated offices in winter, there is the danger of a build-up of static electricity. Semi-conductor devices from which modern computers are constructed, are extremely vulnerable to high voltage discharges. (In a particular office environment, people walked across a carpeted floor to collect their work as it was produced by the printer they all shared. Three printers failed in one day before anyone realised that by simply walking across the carpet the users became charged with enough static to cause the trouble.) Anti-static sprays, anti-static carpeting, discharge mats and, most importantly, changes to working practices can all help to guard against such problems.

Mains supply

A poorly regulated or 'dirty' mains supply can sometimes be the cause of equipmental malfunction which is often hard to trace. Heavy lifts, welding equipment and industrial machinery can cause sudden changes in the mains voltage. If these changes are too great, and the power to the computer is taken from the same supply, then strange things can happen. Screen displays can be distorted, keyboards can become locked and data on disks can be corrupted. The act of switching on a microwave oven in another room has been known to stop a computer from working – much to the annoyance of a programmer who did not save his work often enough. To find out the actual cause will often involve monitoring the situation over a period of time. It is best to keep a log of such problems. Just a note in the diary showing the time, what job the computer was doing, what went wrong and any external conditions that changed at about the same time (e.g. someone plugged in a kettle).

So if you find that your system 'locks up' or 'goes down' for inexplicable reasons, there is a chance that the mains supply is to blame, particularly if you share a building with other companies. One way of overcoming problems with the mains supply is to install a regulator. However, they are expensive, but if you have chosen your suppliers well, you may find that they are willing to loan or rent you one for a short period so that you can find out whether or not you really need one. If you are sure that the problem is being brought into your premises because you share the electricity supply then you can get the electricity company to install a 'clean line'. This requires a separate cable from the point where their cable enters the building to your meter, so you will have to convince them that it is really necessary. They may need to install a recording device to monitor the voltage for two or three weeks to verify the need.

9

Abuse

The technology of hard disk systems requires that the disk be spinning at about 3,000 revolutions per minute and that the recording heads, which are mounted on long arms, be thrust back and forwards over the disk surface whilst remaining very close to it. Any serious knock can cause the arms to vibrate. If the vibration is too great, then the recording heads can come into contact with the surface of the disk and, because the disk is spinning so fast, the magnetic material will be ploughed off and the disk will be damaged. Rapid movement of the computer cabinet can cause gyroscopic effects that distort the disk itself with similar consequences. However, one should not get too alarmed about these dangers because these movements and knocks would have to be pretty severe for problems to occur. Nevertheless, a busy London firm of solicitors found themselves without their file server for several days because staff did not respect the system. The file server was placed beside the desk of a VDU operator who used to place her feet on it when she turned around to chat with her colleague. As she turned back and forth, the cabinet would tilt and knock against the wall. The poor machine stood up to it for several months, but the day came when it got a harder knock than usual and the result was a £1,500 bill for a new disk.

Coffee, tea, soft drinks, confectionery, sandwiches, fruit and other food and drink do not mix well with computing equipment. The most vulnerable items are the keyboard, floppy disks and printers because these are the items that people handle, but it is not unknown for monitors and machines to suffer. The only way to ensure that these problems never occur is to insist that food and drink are kept away from the equipment. However, in a small office this can be difficult to enforce. If it is possible to provide a table and a couple of chairs specifically for the staff to use during their coffee breaks, then the risks can be kept within bounds.

Keeping the user happy

Working with a computer can be extremely demanding. A skilled word processor operator does not have to look at the screen while typing, but what has been entered must be proof-read and this requires concentration to ensure that it is done properly. A greater level of concentration is required to ensure accurate entry of accounting or other critical numerical data. Most people find they get tired after looking at a computer screen for an hour or so.

There are many things that can influence the effectiveness of an operator. Most have been well documented and guidelines have been drawn up by such bodies as the EEC Commission and by trades unions. These guidelines are based on the fact that jobs that entail the concentrated use of VDU screens and keyboards leave little scope for exercise of any kind.

Posture

Prolonged inactivity in any position will eventually lead to discomfort. Poorly designed chairs, badly placed screens and awkward keyboards can quickly lead to long term aches and pains, so it is worthwhile considering the comfort of the operator. Adjustable chairs or stools which incorporate footrests and proper back support will go a long way to help. There should be adequate space on desks to accommodate both keyboards and screens. In particular, the depth of the desks should be sufficient to allow the screens to be placed at viewing distances that the operators find comfortable. Height of the screen is another important factor. The common practice of placing screens on top of computer cabinets often leaves them too high, especially for anyone who wears bifocals. The need to look upwards, in turn, encourages users to slouch down in their chairs. Proper height, slope and overall design of keyboards can help reduce fatigue and thereby cut down keying errors. Most people find that being able to rest forearms on the desk or chair arms is helpful. Again, sufficient depth to desks is important.

The more demanding the work the sooner fatigue sets in. It is therefore necessary to encourage the operators to take short breaks to keep them properly alert. One way of ensuring that this happens is to build in time away from the workstation as part of the job. For instance, accounting and stock control work can be collected into batches to be filed by the operator immediately after having been entered into the computer. Schemes of this type can also be of significant value when tracing dubious entries.

There is considerable variation in personal preference, and so the more flexibility that is built into the arrangements from the start, the easier it will be to accommodate people with different tastes.

Setting up the screen

There are external factors that can affect the performance of the operator. One of the most pernicious is reflections of bright lights and objects on the screen. These can simply be annoying or they can actually affect the readability of the display. It is usually impossible to eliminate reflections altogether, but it is necessary to place the screens, shade lights, adjust curtains, etc., to cut them to a minimum. There are screens or attachments available which can help in stubborn cases.

An often neglected factor is the background behind the screen. Probably the worst thing that one can have is a large, south facing window glazed with reeded glass which can disperse the sun's rays in all directions. Poorly shaded lights or a lot of movement are also undesirable. The best would be a background of about the same brightness as the average over the screen.

The controls on VDUs are often wildly out of adjustment. Very often the screens are run at too high a brightness level which can quickly tire the eyes and wear out the screen. VDU brightness should be adjusted according to the ambient lighting conditions. Operators should be taught what effect each of the knobs on the VDU has on the display and should be encouraged to set them to their own preference. The fact is that many operators just accept the displays as they are installed, but by encouraging them to think about the appearance of the display and showing them how to make adjustments, management can help to make their employees more comfortable. Occasional cleaning with anti-static cleaner can also help.

Displays should be carefully examined when they are first set up after delivery and any that exhibit permanent flicker or movement should be rejected during installation and should be replaced or repaired as quickly as possible. Particular attention should be paid to the top and left-hand side where many activities start.

Amber-coloured screens are recommended by many organisations as being the least liable to produce eye strain.

Hazards

Computers, just like anything that takes its power from the electrical mains supply, are potentially a source of electric shock. However, all potentially dangerous areas of these machines have been manufactured under strict controls and with safety as a paramount consideration. Even with the lid off no dangerous voltages will be exposed unless there is a warning to the contrary. All lethal voltage sources will be confined to the power supply module. (An exception can be the VDU monitor which should be left well alone.)

At one time there was a 'radiation' scare with some alarmist reports in the press concerning dangers for computer users and VDU operators. 'Radiation' conjures up fears and apprehension because it is associated with the nuclear industry, because much of it is invisible and because so few people understand anything about it. Let it be made clear that the radiations or emissions associated with computer equipment that is working normally are of a different nature or quality. Potentially the most serious emission is that of X-rays which are produced wherever the screen is bright. However, the energy (destructive power) of these X-rays is negligible compared with those we submit ourselves to at the dentist.

We are surrounded by natural radiation at all times. Some of it is harmful. Generally speaking, it is impossible or impractical to protect ourselves from it.

Trade unions have a legitimate interest in protecting their members, but may also attempt to exploit opportunities for substantial improvements in their working conditions which are not called for by the safety requirements.

Noise

Most computers have a fan in them which runs all the time – although there are systems that monitor the temperature of the equipment and adjust the speed to suit. Hard disks must rotate continuously to ensure that the data is available to the user at all times. The motors and moving parts for these devices are sometimes noisy enough to intrude and tire the user. Impact printers such as daisy wheels and dot matrix machines can be excessively noisy and can even cause annoying vibration when placed on or near a user's desk. Judicious placement of such equipment within the office and cushioning (without obstructing ventilation slots) can effectively alleviate these problems. Ink-jet and laser printers have effectively replaced daisy wheel machines, most of which required proper (and costly) acoustic hoods for silencing. Dot matrix printers are likely to be with us for some time to come because they are so cheap to buy and run.

Cabling

A basic stand alone machine can have as many as six or seven external cables associated with it. Add a mouse, plotter, modem, etc., and the number will more than double. It is desirable to keep these cables under control to avoid putting excessive strain on the connectors and on the sockets on the equipment. Cable lengths can severely limit the relative positioning of the various parts of the system. Cables should always have a little slack in them to allow for movement, but excess cable should be neatly coiled and tied to prevent it from becoming a hazard waiting to trip someone. There is no ideal solution to the problem, but it might be worthwhile investigating the availability of computer workstation desks with specially designed trunking to carry cables.

A system with several independently powered pieces of machinery will need the same number of power points for connection to the mains. The best solution is to have sufficient wall outlets put in by an electrician, but it is possible to install do-it-yourself trunking that can be plugged into a mains socket. A temporary arrangement is possible with 'blocks of four' extension leads, but these must be used with all safety considerations taken into account. One of the above-mentioned workstation desks with built-in mains wiring could solve the problem. There is little chance that a single workstation, even with a couple of printers and additional items, would begin to overload a mains lead because modern electronic equipment takes very little power.

With networking and multi-user systems, the cabling requirements must be considered together with the equipment. The routeing of the signal cables should be discussed in detail with a representative of the supplier or cabling contractor. Ducting should generally be installed, but it is a moot point whether or not to lay and prepare the cables themselves before the equipment arrives as it nearly always happens that users want to make adjustments and move the equipment a few feet or so when they see the new working environment. Problems with crowding and cabling in the vicinity of workstations are reduced, because many devices can be shared via the central controller. Connection to the mains can often be made by a single cable because VDUs can be fitted with cables that take power from the rear of the computer. The network signal cable will either come direct from the file server or will loop through a connector at the back of the computer. Multi-user systems nearly always require a separate signal cable between each terminal and the central processing unit.

10 Staff training

The basic system □ Housekeeping □ Commands □
Networks and multi-user systems □ Dealing with malfunctions
□ Applications □ Training methods □ Non-supervisory
training

There are two aspects of staff training with regard to computer systems. First of all, there is the body of common knowledge of the basic system that all users should be familiar with: how to get it going, what to do when things don't seem to be working properly, what precautions to take against losing data. Second, individuals will need to have a special knowledge of the applications software they will be using.

The basic system

Most users in a small business should be sufficiently familiar with the basic control of the computer system that they do not have to refer to, or rely on, someone else to help them get it going, shut it down, look after their own security or cope with minor problems. These activities should be included in the initial training – at least two staff members should be made familiar with them all. Young people who have gained experience of computers are coming onto the market in ever increasing numbers. However, there is no standard body of knowledge with which they will all be familiar. Schools have, unfortunately, not moved quickly enough to take up business standard microcomputers, and school-leavers will generally need further training.

Housekeeping

Everyone who uses your computer should be prepared to make sure all cables are properly located and that all plugs are pushed fully home. They should know the location of all switches both at the wall and on their terminals, the printers and any other equipment that they use. They should also be aware of the settings of these switches for correct operation of the system. Other routine mechanical activities that should be common knowledge include how to insert a floppy disk, how to load paper into a printer, how to change a ribbon, possibly how to change the toner cartridge in an ink-jet or laser printer.

Commands

When the computer is switched on, it must be provided with a program to follow. This is usually supplied from a hard disk or from a floppy. Some systems require that a specially prepared floppy (a 'key' disk) be inserted into a particular drive for correct operation to ensue. The key disk can be set up to call in a particular applications program so that you can start work immediately. Your supplier would have to set up special little programs to hide the rather cryptic system commands from you. In this way your choice would be limited, which can be extremely useful from the point of view of security.

You may want greater freedom because the computer is an extremely versatile piece of machinery. It is controlled by a set of commands that are usually entered from the keyboard, and knowledge of a small set of these commands can be extremely useful. They will only work at the operating system level, that is, without any active applications program in your machine and this includes so-called 'front end shells' which are environments specially designed to hide the operating system from the user. If you have such a shell, it will usually include an option to exit to the operating system. If you choose to work at the operating system level you should be warned that it can be hostile and you should equip yourself with star chart, compass, waterbottle and clothing for all climates. Moreover, it is possible for you to do serious damage to your system.

A complete set of commands will be listed in your operating system manual with explanations of their purposes and a short guide is included in Appendix 4. Most commands are abbreviations of their purpose. For instance, DIR is short for 'Directory' and CD is short for 'Change Directory'. The first of these is completely benign and cannot affect the performance of your system. The second is also benign in respect of the system, but it can affect the way it is perceived from your terminal. In the first instance it is best to avoid those that write to disk, the one exception being a new floppy disk. There should be someone in most departments of your business who knows how to format a floppy disk, how to take security copies and how to retrieve data from these copies.

Networks and multi-user systems

Networks and multi-user systems generally require a little more user response before they become active, and every user should know how to log into the system, how to choose the application they need and how to log out when they have completed their work. An additional level of security is necessary with networking and multi-user systems to prevent unauthorised access to sensitive data. For instance, you would not want the typing pool or the warehouse to have access to the nominal ledger. This additional security is provided by means of user names and passwords which can control and limit the access available to that terminal.

Dealing with malfunctions

From time to time all mechanical systems cease to function properly. A computer is no exception. Faults can occur in the hardware, in the software, in the files. It is not always easy, even for an expert, to distinguish where the fault lies. The trick is to ensure that the failure does not become a disaster. The first step is to recognise when something is wrong because some faults can creep in unnoticed. The initial training of the staff should include some guidance in these matters.

Any change in the response of the system should be reported immediately and no further work carried out until it is certain that there is nothing wrong. Faults that give rise to error messages on the screen should be logged because the message could be the key to quick repair. In the early days of operation of a system there are likely to be some false alarms until people become familiar with its peculiarities. A chain of command should be put in place, ultimately ending up with the supplier, or maintenance company.

Potentially the most serious faults can occur with historical data processing applications such as accounts. If ever anything appears amiss with such a system, no further processing should take place until it is clear what has happened. Missing transactions or a balance not agreeing with the total of transactions should be viewed with alarm and a course of remedial action put into operation immediately. Verify carefully that what has apparently occurred is indeed the case. If it is, then the data on the machine is corrupt and should be replaced with the latest security copy (back-up) which should, in turn, be scrutinised to ensure that it does not also contain the error. If it is correct then work can continue, but it should be borne in mind that any entries made since the security copies were taken will be absent and must be re-entered. If the error persists, earlier security copies must be loaded until an error-free version is found and then all subsequent entries will have to be repeated.

Applications

Except for the more common packages or proprietory software it is unreasonable to expect your supplier to be able to provide training for every application you need. A commonly used and generally successful method is to contract a third party. If the introduction of the computer system is properly planned, there may be time to take advantage of short courses which are becoming progressively more common at local colleges.

In all subjects you will find terminology (jargon) and methods of working that will be common knowledge to those working in the field. A computer with quality software will usually follow these methods and incorporate jargon as a matter of course. Anyone familiar with computers and with the subject will be able to use and understand the workings of the software, although there might be a few contentious areas. Someone who lacks experience of the subject will often find the software incomprehensible and difficult to use. Training is essential for the efficient use of applications packages.

A small supplier of beauty products purchased a computer and integrated software for accounts and stock control. The salesman recommended that he should spend another £150 on training (a figure that works out at less than 5 per cent of the cost of the system), but he adamantly refused. Three months later, and after blaming the computer, the software, the mains supply, his assistants, the salesman and the supplier, he came to realise how much grief he could have saved himself had he spent the extra money. When the reality of the situation finally dawned on him and he realised just how much time he had wasted, he offered to be a referee and to recommend to any purchasers the benefits, indeed the necessity, of training.

Training methods

There are many ways in which users can become more aware of both the applications they are using and computing in general. If you or your staff have no experience at all, then it may make a good deal of sense to attend one of the short courses in computer appreciation which are commonly available at technical colleges or adult education centres. Such a course will give people new to computers direct experience of how computers work and what they might be capable of doing. However, for the purpose of running a business, you may well require more directly related training for your own specific needs.

Package training courses are available from a whole host of companies as well as colleges. Such courses can normally be arranged on your own premises or at a training centre. If training is specially arranged for your needs on your own business premises, then you can expect to pay more for this extra convenience. You should make sure that wherever the training is held:

1. it should be directly related to your requirements. For example, there is little point in spending money having an operator trained in word processing using Wordstar Professional Version 5 when you are using Multimate Advantage II for word processing.
2. it is at the right time. If you train staff on any package six months before you propose to use it, they may well have forgotten some of the skills or left the business. In the case of packages where many modules have to be implemented, then training can always be arranged over a longer period of time as and when needed.
3. the person(s) conducting the training is (are) qualified in some way to do the job. Do not allow yourself or your staff to be trained by someone inexperienced at training. However well someone knows a product, it does not make them good at training.
4. it is pitched at the right level for your requirements and for your staff. Many training providers offer differing levels of course such as beginners, intermediate and advanced. Remember that there may be no need to develop advanced skills in a package if your business is not going to use the package at such a level. In many cases, you may well put staff in different level courses according to their ability and needs.

10

5. it is carried out on similar hardware to your own. If staff are taught to use a package on one machine and then work on a different machine there can be a problem. This can only occur if training is done away from the business and insufficient support material is provided such as reference guides and course notes. Even after training has been completed, it is unlikely that all aspects of a package that have been taught will be applied straightaway. The support material can be used to help users remember how to perform certain functions later on in their work.

Non-supervisory training

This training can be supplemented or replaced by different kinds of training. In other words, training that does not necessarily require supervision. Although such methods are normally slower ways of learning and sometimes less thorough, they can be done exactly when needed and at a pace better suited to the individual's needs and taste.

Computer Based training (CBT) is such an example. Essentially, the user is taught by the computer. The computer is used to display information and instructions and is able to respond to a user's reply. The computer can then guide users through the use of a package, monitoring their understanding and proficiency in the use of the package. Users can then work through the training as and when they wish and at any pace. Some such techniques even incorporate video equipment (interactive video) to support the training program, so instructions and displays are illustrated on video to assist the learning program.

Finally, there is always the use of the manuals that come with the software and books that are now available for most of the leading packages. This do-it-yourself approach is by far the cheapest way of developing skills and understanding of the package, but is also the hardest.

11 Implementing an applications package

The problem □ Deciding when to start □ Getting yourself prepared □ On to the computer □ Up and going! □ Changing software needs

In this chapter, we are going to consider the work involved in setting up business data processing systems which are ongoing and rely on accurate historical data for correct operation. This is in contrast to applications such as calculations of the strength of a span of a bridge, where the computer is used mainly as a calculating machine and where all the data required to produce the final result is available at the start of operations.

The problem

If you are starting a new business there will be no history of financial transactions, stock acquisitions or distributions, no maintenance records, etc. You know that you are just about to open a new bank account. You have only just started negotiating with suppliers. You have not yet invoiced any customers. The data on which the software relies will start to be accrued from day one and can be entered into the computer as it becomes available. Actually, this precise situation is rare. The real point is that, say, three weeks ago your enterprise did not exist and so all balances were zero and it is easy to remember what happened to the money and where the stock came from.

A fully operational business with a busy daily routine is an entirely different matter. There are likely to be bad debts. Suppliers will owe you credit notes. A cheque stub may be blank or illegible. Invoices may be missing. Purchase orders might not be filed correctly. VAT may have been calculated incorrectly. A customer may have paid only part of an invoice. And petty cash probably does not reconcile. You will probably have to work for an entire weekend to find out how much working capital the business currently commands and even then your answer will not be very accurate.

In short, an active accounts system is likely to be chaotic. The same applies to other record keeping activities. You will be lucky if you have had time to keep the chaos under control.

Unless there has been strict discipline and careful attention to detail during the lifetime of the business, then there are likely to be errors in the books. Record keeping activities are non-productive. You will neglect them to attend to the more urgent jobs that crowd in on you. After all, you did not set up your business simply to have a perfect set of accounts, but to sell your products or services to your customers and to make a profit. However, you find that a chunk of your profit goes to pay your bookkeeper and those big bills from your accountants take what is left.

Deciding when to start

The computer system (and that includes the software) should be acquired at least three months before the changeover is to take place. This will give time for people to become familiar with the operation of both the computer and the software. It will also give you a chance to assess the reliability of the equipment and to solve teething problems.

We will assume that your computer system has been delivered with the accounts and/or stock control packages properly installed, but containing no entries. You should take a back-up of the empty working files at this stage, write-protect them and store them away for safekeeping. It is a good plan to do this before the supplier has left your premises after installation so that you can get immediate help. By doing this, if something goes wrong with the system, or if you make a mess of entering the data, then you can restore the original clean files. You might like to experiment with the system and get familiar with its peculiarities before you actually load 'live' data, but remember to restore the clean files before starting work in earnest.

Getting yourself prepared

Setting up a computerised record keeping system while a business is in operation calls for a great deal of work. It cannot be done overnight. Plans should be set in motion at least six months in advance. Effort should be directed at ensuring the accuracy and completeness of the present manual system. It would probably be worth the expense of having your accountant draw up a trial balance for you at the end of the year. A month or so before changeover, static information should be entered: e.g. for an accounting function, names, addresses and other details of customers and suppliers together with the nominal account names and codes can be keyed in. Take a new backup of the files with zero balances at this time. Protect and store them away carefully as it might be easier to start with completely empty balances if problems arise when numerical data has been entered.

Your accountant should be briefed early and requested to prepare a trial balance for your business soon after the end of your financial year. (A small supplier of beauty products sorely regretted not having paid his accountant for this service when, after struggling for three months he still could not get his system working properly.)

On to the computer

At the end of the financial year, all the balances should be struck on the manual books and transferred to the ready-prepared accounts on the computer. Now is the time to print out a trial balance. If you have a trial balance from your accountant then the two should agree; if not, the chances are it will not balance and effort will have to be expended to find out where the errors are. Do not proceed until a balance has been achieved. Make another back-up at this stage as these files represent a starting point in the history of the system. (If the errors cannot be found in a reasonable time, then suspense accounts must be set up to make it balance. Transfers can then be made to or from the suspense account as and when the errors come to light.) Remember that your regular manual record keeping will have to be continued until the computer system proves to be doing its job properly.

In the case of a stock control system, the supplier details and stock types should be entered in plenty of time. When the end-of-year physical stock taking has been completed, the amount of each type of stock can be entered. The entry of all stock movements that take place thereafter should then cause the totals to agree with the physical totals. Lack of agreement will signal either errors in the record keeping or that there has been a shrinkage in stock.

Ideally much of this work is carried out at the end of the business's financial year and the records should be available at that time. What is required is a 'snapshot' of the state of the business at a known time. However, unless proper preparations have been made, the historical nature of record keeping and the delays imposed by auditing procedures dictate that there may be two or three months' work outstanding before it is possible to start entering transactions into the computer.

Up and going!

In this light, a computer system serves several purposes. First of all, it enforces a discipline that is likely to have been missing from the manual system. Errors in the records can be highlighted in a matter of seconds. Time consuming calculations and many hand-written documents are no longer necessary. The computer becomes the controlling force in the record keeping activities. Second, it deskills the record keeping job. Almost anyone who can press keys on a keyboard can be trained to operate at least parts of the system. Thus many people can help. Third, jobs that formerly required several distinct activities will now be done completely by the computer which will keep the records as it performs other tasks. For instance, raising an invoice on the computer will ensure that names are spelt consistently, that credit levels are not exceeded, that calculations are accurate, that all the appropriate monetary values are adjusted. Fourth, you will be able to send a complete and accurate set of accounts for your accountants to audit. Their job will be easier. They will be able to do it quicker and their bills should be reduced accordingly.

In the case of a well designed stock control system, there will be automatic warnings of low stock levels, highlighting of slow or fast moving product lines and up-to-date stock valuation at any time. You should be able to list the suppliers of a particular product together with prices and discount rates and so be in a stronger position when negotiating for better discount as your business expands. Of course, mistakes will be made and there might be shrinkage from various causes, but the computer will show how much of each product there should be and investigations can be put in train to find out the cause of shortages. Knowledge that there can be a check at any time can have a salutary effect on staff honesty!

Changing software needs

It is inevitable that once a computer system has been set up, your computer needs will change. In many ways, extending a system is very much easier than changing what it has to do.

One need for change may arise as a result of wanting to acquire an upgraded version of a particular software package. If this occurs, you may well find that the new version of the software is unable to read the information generated and stored by the previous one. In most cases, a new version will come with programs that will convert this information into a form that can be read by the new programs.

If information has to be converted to (say) 3.5 inch disks from 5.25 inch, then you can get the data crossed over. You will not need to start from the beginning simply because the type of storage medium your business uses changes.

In some cases you may wish to convert your business to using a completely different set of software. In this instance, you should seek advice about how you can get your existing data converted. There are very few cases where data conversion in these circumstances cannot be done.

If your firm has used software especially written or tailored for it ('bespoke' software), then adapting software for the changing needs of your business can be an ongoing activity and an integral part of running the system.

11

12 A further case study

The facts □ Background □ Getting started □ Crisis
management □ Getting settled □ Expanding the system

This case study is based on Paperlot Stationery Supplies, an
imaginary stationery firm that supplies stationery through one retail
outlet and distributes supplies to a large number of companies and
individuals. The firm has three categories of customers:

1. **Customers through its retail outlet.**
2. **Corporate organisations who are supplied in bulk and receive
   sizable discounts.**
3. **Small firms and individuals who order goods based on a widely
   distributed mail order catalogue.**

Although at the time of the study this firm had a large customer
base, its supplier base was relatively small, three large UK based
firms and about fifteen overseas companies who supplied to the firm
via UK based agents; this avoided Paperlot having to handle
importing procedures.

The facts

The following facts will help give some perspective on the
company.

Number of employees:

Retail staff		2
Driving and dispatch		2
Storekeeper		1
Administrative		2
Managerial		1
	Total staff	8

Turnover	£2.4 million
Expected number of orders	250 per month

Number of suppliers	18
Number of regular customers – corporate	26
mail order	800
Average stock value on premises	£150,000
Number of different items held in stock	2,000

Background

The business developed over four years of trading and was founded by its manager, Jack Staples. The business grew rapidly. The mail order side of the business, the latest part of its activity, had been launched one year before.

Staples envisaged that the retailing and corporate sides of the business would grow less than 5 per cent per annum over the following three years. On the other hand, if it could get its marketing and distribution right, the mail order side could double over the following two years.

In order to develop the mail order side of the business, Staples believed that the sales side of the business would need to be computerised in order to cope with the growth in administrative activity.

Getting started

Staples took the following actions:

1. He organised national newspaper and magazine advertising of his catalogues. The advertisements were designed to coincide in all publications in one month's time.
2. He ordered from his printers a new set of catalogues.
3. He bought a microcomputer with a 20 Mbyte hard disk, a colour screen and a printer. The microcomputer was one of the latest and looked extremely stylish; he was always fussy about appearance.
4. He purchased an accounts package containing sales and purchase ledger, nominal ledger and sales invoicing, through a dealer. He learnt about this package from an accountant friend at his golf club who used a computer for his business accounts.

12

After receiving delivery of the computer hardware and software, Staples spent many hours struggling with the manuals to get the system set up and installed. Eventually, with a little help from a friend and a few phone calls to the dealers who sold him the computer system and the software, he managed it.

After two weeks of having the system, he decided to appoint one of his administration staff to operate the new system; Judy Punch. Judy was sent on a three-day course to learn about the packages. Because the course did not exactly start when he needed it, four weeks had passed before Judy started the course. This coincided with the advertisements for the mail order. On top of the normal business load, Judy was on a three-day course and requests for 3,000 catalogues had suddenly accumulated. All staff were now working overtime in order to get the catalogues delivered, with some orders from existing customers being held up for a day or two.

When Judy returned from her course she was required to set up the system with a view to implementing the sales ledger immediately to incorporate the new customer accounts on the mail order side of the business. Judy spent many hours setting the sales ledger up and entering all the customer details for existing mail order customers. The time spent doing this meant further neglect of other processing activities in the firm; again orders were being delayed, this time because invoices were not being set up correctly.

Crisis management

After another two weeks, new customer orders were coming in at about ninety a day; the administration could not cope. Staples, in a state of near panic, contacted the local job agency and recruited two temporary staff to help handle requests for catalogues, production of invoices and some basic accounts work for the shop. In addition to this, he employed the services of a consultant from a neighbouring firm who was experienced at setting up computerised systems for such firms.

With the help of two temporary staff, who needed a good deal of supervision, and a consultant, a plan of action was drawn up.

The two staff in the shop concentrated on managing the shop and doing something about getting the backlog of work sorted out. Many stocks were low in the shop by now and disgruntled customers were complaining of some stocks not being available. In addition to this, some accounts work had been neglected.

The two temporary staff and the other administrator concentrated on getting the mail order and corporate customer orders backlog sorted. This largely involved getting orders processed and invoices made up so that goods could be dispatched.

The storekeeper and drivers concentrated on coping with the extra dispatches. A larger proportion of dispatches had to be sent by post in order to cope with the extra work.

During all this activity, Judy Punch was able to get the sales ledger set up properly and enter all invoices through the sales ledger. By the end of the second month, the processing was up to date and customers received their first computerised set of statements of account.

Getting settled

It was difficult to assess whether any real lasting damage had been caused by the introduction of a computer and the transition period that occurred, but Staples felt certain that some ground had been lost with some of the firm's mail order customers, and orders were lost with two large corporate customers. In addition to that, Staples spent a good deal of money employing staff for overtime, employing temporary staff and paying consultancy fees. It is also certain that his advertising campaign to expand the mail order side of the business did not have the impetus it was designed to have.

However, in spite of everything, growth in business activity was expected, albeit not as large as originally planned. With the help of the consultant he hired, the decision was made to start the nominal ledger as soon as staff training was adequate. One of the shop staff was trained on the system along with Staples himself.

Meanwhile, one of the temporary staff left the firm and the other took on full-time status with the company; Staples felt the growth in the mail order side of the business now justified the extra member of staff.

Once the training was over, the decision was made to set up and run the nominal ledger. On this occasion, the transition went smoothly. It only took a few days to set up the accounts and enter the opening balances. Staples learnt from previous experience and from the training course that adequate planning and preparation were important factors when converting manual files to computerised ones.

It soon became evident that the system, with only one microcomputer, was not sufficient for the business information requirements. He was advised to install a network of three microcomputers. Consequently, he needed two extra microcomputers and a file server. The new system was set up with two computers placed in the main office and one with the storekeeper for future

12

development. Staples regretted not being able to anticipate this early on because the adaptation to a network cost more than would normally be necessary and it meant having to retrain staff for the different skills required of them. It also caused a little staff resentment.

Very soon after this, both shop workers had got used to the computerised system and found that it was saving them time. Also, Staples had learnt how to extract the information he wanted from the ledgers and was soon planning effectively for changes in sales and keeping closer tags on customer debt.

The consultant informed Staples that the total cost of the implementation to date probably cost him 50 per cent more than it should have if he had gone about it in the right way early on.

Expanding the system

After two months, the system had settled well and Staples was ready to computerise the purchase ledger, sales order processing, invoicing and purchase ordering activities of his company. He sent his storekeeper on a course with the aim of learning how to set up and maintain the product files needed for the operation of the additional software.

As soon as the storekeeper felt ready, he began to prepare the stock records by ensuring that all stock cards were complete and accurate. It was decided that stores would be kept separate from the shop. When goods were moved from stores to shop, it would be treated as a stock issue from stores in much the same way as issuing stock to customers through mail order. The storekeeper converted all records to the computer in about one month and soon learnt to keep the records updated, especially with prices.

A major problem occurred because Judy Punch left the firm for another job; she felt that with so much computing expertise behind her she could command a much higher salary than Staples was willing to offer. Staples had to recruit another employee to bring him to full staff strength. Finding another member of staff with the necessary expertise proved difficult. Eventually he found someone, after increasing the salary offered by 20 per cent. This new person still needed training and some time to be able to get to grips with the way Paperlot went about its business.

The transition period between Judy leaving and the new person taken on being able to work fully went on for about two months. During this period, some potential trade was lost along with some credibility with many customers. Unfortunately the usual backlog of work had built up. Staff morale had also taken a little knock.

It took nearly three months for the expanded system to settle finally and for all the data processing to be brought up to date. Much of the management information was only just becoming of real use to Staples.

After one year of activity, Paperlot had expanded its business on all activities, especially the mail order aspect. Staples, on reflection, felt that computerisation was a success but realised that it could have gone much better with more careful planning, better handling of the staffing situation and better use of informed advice.

12

PART FOUR

The next steps

This part attempts to answer the question, 'What happens next?' It covers a number of topics including regular procedures to ensure an efficient and secure system, where to get support when difficulties are encountered, and what to do when things go wrong.

Extending the system is discussed, including both doing more things and doing more of the same.

The concluding chapter uses a case study as a way of illustrating most of the issues raised in this book and as means of placing such issues into a business context.

13 Looking after your system

Maintenance □ Security

Maintenance

Like any other piece of machinery, a computer needs to be looked after and repaired from time to time. There will be a warranty period of ninety days during which you can expect to have any inherent faults corrected free of charge. When the warranty runs out, you will be on your own unless you arrange for your maintenance to be carried out for you by an external company.

Type of service

You must decide what kind of service you need or are willing or able to pay for. The better the service you need, the more you can expect to pay. You could opt for an *ad hoc* call-out service which you would only call upon when something actually goes wrong, or you could opt to pay for an engineer to be on your premises all the time ready to repair after breakdown and to perform pre-emptive servicing. It is clear that the latter will be expensive, but there are serious drawbacks to the former. In between these two approaches there is a variety of standard insurance and maintenance schemes from which you can choose. These will have specified response times and clauses relating to labour and hardware costs.

Ideally, of course, you would like your system to be operational at all times, but, as with your car, it will occasionally fail you. With a computer system the failures are likely to be much more abrupt and can happen without any warning at all. So, how long can you continue without the use of your computer? How long will it take you to catch up when the system is repaired? How much will it cost you in lost income and overtime payments? Can you make other arrangements to tide you over the crisis? The type of maintenance contract you finally choose will depend upon your assessment of your situation.

13

A standard, middle of the road, maintenance contract will set you back between 10 and 15 per cent of the equipment costs and will specify a response time of eight working hours. This means that an engineer will be on your premises next day at latest. It does not mean that your system will be up and running in that time. If you want a faster response time, then the cost will rise fairly steeply because it means that the maintenance company will have to employ more engineers and they are not cheap. The contract will usually specify that the maintenance company will use its 'best endeavours' to correct the problem without delay. However, if this involves acquiring special parts from abroad, it can mean that you will have to wait several days or perhaps a week or more. To mitigate the effects of such delays, you may be able to find a contract which entitles you to borrow certain types of equipment while yours is being repaired. Alternatively, you could rent enough to keep the critical parts of your data processing system up to date. If you find a good maintenance company, it is worthwhile building up a rapport with the people involved, acting on their advice, keeping them happy by paying their invoices on time and making sure that they are not called out simply because you haven't switched on at the mains socket. (In fact, calls like that may be subject to standard charges, so read the fine print.)

Performance levels

In large organisations and where reliance upon computer performance is heavy, it is common practice to define acceptable performance levels. Within your contract you can specify a minimum performance level below which the maintenance company will incur penalties. This performance will normally be measured by the percentage of working time possible with your system. It is not unreasonable to expect it to be fully working for at least 95 per cent of the time, i.e. to be unavailable for no more than one day per month. As you make more demands, so the maintenance fees will escalate because you will have to cover the costs of additional personnel or insurance premiums.

You are entitled to have the maintenance company make its best endeavours to keep your system in working order. There may be factors which could result in your system being unavailable for days or weeks. Generally, such a situation would arise if the maintenance company had to order new components from abroad. Delays in deliveries from foreign companies can be substantial. If long delays are totally unacceptable to you then you will have to require the maintenance company to guarantee to get your system working within a given period. The cost of maintenance will be correspondingly greater because you will have to pay for the additional stock required by the maintenance company.

Long term provision of maintenance

Large organisations, for instance, local government departments, often require assurance that computing equipment they buy will be supported for up to seven years in the future. This means that they will have obsolete, worn-out kit at that time and will be looking to major revisions in their systems when the contract expires. A small business, however, would hope to expand substantially in seven years and, by using the roll-over leasing method, adding new equipment and replacing old, it could stay at the forefront of technology and gradually extend its system.

Prices

As we have already seen, it is common for the price of maintenance to be between 10 and 15 per cent of the cost of the hardware per annum, for an average level of service. For critical applications, and where the investment warrants it, higher premiums will be necessary to ensure fast response and availability of engineers. It is unwise to try to cut down on the cost of maintenance unless in-house skills are adequate.

Service

Service can range from permanent, on-site engineers, through two-, four- or eight-hour call-out, to *ad hoc* arrangements. The expense obviously decreases with the service. If you have in-house expertise and a certain amount of redundancy within your computer system, then the *ad hoc* arrangement could be the best for you. However, without such expertise, it could become quite expensive.

Rebates

If the maintenance company is likely to fail to meet its obligations by a wide margin, it might be worthwhile having a penalty or rebate clause in the contract. It could either extend your contract for a given period or penalise the maintenance company to some degree in the event that the quality of service falls below a certain level.

13

Assignment and compatibility

If a particular piece of equipment gives an abnormal amount of trouble, it is quite likely that the maintenance company will exchange parts, such as mother boards, disk drives or power supplies in order to keep your system up and running. During the course of this activity, it is possible that they might downgrade your equipment. Occasionally it might even be upgraded. Most likely this would be done as a matter of expediency, but the unscrupulous company might take advantage of the situation. When such substitutions occur, it is very important to ensure that compatibility with existing equipment is maintained. It is therefore necessary to keep a list of the serial numbers of the equipment and a note of the specifications of each item that you originally purchased. Any questions can then be resolved by reference to the appropriate documents.

You should ascertain whether any maintenance contract you agree with your supplier will be carried out by, or assigned to, a third party. If you elect to change or are forced to change your maintenance company, then you should ensure that the new company performs an initial inspection. (They would want to do so anyway to assess the state of your system before taking on a contract involving used equipment.) You should accompany the new engineer during the inspection and agree the calibre, specifications, and serial numbers of the equipment.

Maintenance log

A maintenance log should be kept to show what faults have occurred, the response times of the maintenance company, the amount of down time, the name of the engineer, the work done by the engineer, the serial numbers and specifications of equipment removed for servicing (and signed for by the engineer), the serial numbers and specifications of substitutions (and signed for by you or a responsible member of your staff). A professional approach to the upkeep of your system will pay dividends, will be duly noted by the maintenance company, and the maintenance log could be a valuable document in the case of disputes.

If there is a history of poor response times and lack of commitment on the part of the maintenance company, you may have legal recourse to them for losses incurred by your business. A well documented report on their performance would provide an excellent starting point.

Security

Vulnerability of computers

The data which a small business will store on its computer contains value from two points of view. Entering data from the keyboard involves cost penalties in the form of wages and overheads and possibly the loss of revenue since labour might be diverted from a money earning activity. Data on the computer therefore has a value simply from being there. It also has value by virtue of the fact that it can be used to commercial advantage by people or organisations with the appropriate knowledge. A list of your customers would be of immediate use to a competitor as would a list of suppliers together with the discounts your business is able to command.

So the data on your computer is an asset to your company. It is not clear whether it is a tangible asset or not. But as an asset it will need looking after. Before you can begin to protect it, you have to recognise the ways in which it can lose value. For instance, it could just vanish. Someone could erase it by accident, or the machine could simply fail and destroy your data as it does so. Someone could erase it maliciously. On the other hand it could still be there, but be so badly corrupted as to be useless. Again, the corruption could be accidental, the result of system failure, or it could be a malicious act. It could still be on your computer, but be inaccessible to you because you have forgotten the encryption code words you were using. It could be copied fraudulently and passed on to a competitor or someone who could benefit from it without any recompense to you.

Failures and corruption can be dealt with by making copies on a regular schedule, but a word of caution is necessary. Corruption of data may not become obvious for days or even weeks and you will have to make sure that the back-up system is working properly. There is always the risk that all recent back-ups are corrupt and so steps must be taken to ensure that you do not have to re-enter too much data when corruption of data is discovered. Accordingly, the following schedule is suggested as a basic scheme that will ensure that you minimise the amount of data that you have to re-enter. You can adapt it to suit your circumstances.

13

Back-up

Entries recorded within a computer system cannot be considered as secure, even after they have been filed. In order to guard against the loss of data or the possibility that computer files might become corrupted beyond repair, it is necessary to back up (make copies of) the files that have been updated. The value of back-up copies will only be fully understood should data be lost as a result of power failure, or one or more of a thousand other unpredictable causes. To avoid the traumatic experience of trying to recover corrupted files, it is essential to make back-up copies regularly and to do this to a consistent, systematic plan.

Back-up copies of your files should be made at least each day after transactions have been entered. A minimum of three sets of clearly labelled media (floppy disks or tapes), which could be used over a long period, should provide adequate safety, providing they are used systematically. One set should be used for Mondays and Wednesdays; a second set for Tuesdays and Thursdays; the third set for Fridays. (The actual scheme adopted may reasonably differ from the one suggested, depending upon the volume of postings or other particular circumstances.)

In addition, permanent back-ups should be taken prior to running monthly, or periodic, routines that reset values within the files. These back-ups should be stored safely either in a fire-proof safe or away from the premises.

It is important that back-up should be made only if there is no suspicion of error in the data files on the hard disk. If any report or batch list shows a fault that might be attributable to an error in the files on the hard disk, then the regular backup media should not be used, but immediately write-protected and placed in a safe location. The problem with the data files must be resolved before proceeding to enter any more transactions. If the apparent errors are not caused by file corruption, then the regular back-up schedule can be reinstated, otherwise it might be necessary to restore the files to an earlier state from the most recent back-ups. Again these should be checked for integrity, reverting to even earlier back-ups if they are also faulty. If errors are caught quickly, then it should be possible to resume with data no more than a couple of days old.

Periodically, say once a month, a set of back-ups should be write-protected, labelled and filed away just in case a deep-seated error comes to light. Also it is sometimes useful to be able to refer to archived material, particularly if, say, monthly routines reset values within the files.

Passwords

To avoid forgetting passwords you should use words that have some meaning to you – such as your grandmother's maiden name. To improve security, you should change passwords from time to time. When you do this, remember that your backup copies may still depend upon an old password. Good encryption code words are usually longer and it is a good idea to use a quotation from a piece of poetry, perhaps spelling one of the words incorrectly.

It is important to be aware of the ways in which information can be extracted from computers and the fact that it can be done without leaving any trace of the machine having been disturbed. If people have access to your computer, any one of them could find out where you store data they might find of value and make copies onto floppy disks. Copying a list of a thousand names and addresses would take no more than two or three minutes. A more subtle approach would be for someone to take your back-up disks (possibly substituting another set to avoid rousing suspicion) to copy them in the evening and to return them to their normal place first thing next morning. A combination of unscrupulous competitor and disloyal employee could be disastrous for the wellbeing of your business.

Where security is lax a computer system will be vulnerable to various forms of danger. Accidents, unwitting contamination, malicious meddling, fraudulent tampering and the introduction of computer viruses can be the result. Unauthorised access to computer files can be extremely damaging because data can be tampered with, falsified, erased or otherwise affected. Serious cases of such activity have even led to bankruptcies.

If you have a stand alone computer, it should not be tucked away so that someone can get access to it without anyone else being aware. If you can keep it under lock and key when you are not in the office then you can retain control, but at the expense of preventing the machine from being used to full advantage. Passwords help to a certain extent by preventing a casual user from gaining access to your programs and some files, but they cannot prevent files from being copied and perused at leisure from another machine. Data encryption (encoding) is recommended for sensitive documents since it can be a very effective method of rendering them unreadable. However, it does carry a penalty in that it can take a substantial amount of time to save and recall such documents.

Security of hardware

In addition to computers, most businesses will have other valuable equipment on their premises. Therefore it makes sense to have an alarm system that guards against intruders when the staff are not

13

present. Most insurers will insist upon such arrangements and it is wise to keep a written list of serial numbers of all the office equipment you have. You will have to judge whether an opportunist would be able to make off with any of your computers during the day. If you have one in the front office, then it might be worthwhile investing in a locking device that clamps the machine firmly to the desk. Security markings and stickers can also act as deterrents.

Network security

Networks and multi-user systems have serious implications for security, but they have all of necessity been addressed by their builders in one way or another. By their very nature, such systems need to control access from any terminal attached to them. They require the user to be identified and can request a password to improve security. Control can be exercised by allowing only identified users to have access and then to allow such users access to only selected parts of the system and with no means of making copies of any major part of any large file. All accesses can be logged and any attempts at security violation should be brought to the immediate attention of the supervisor. All access to sensitive files should be logged so that it can be traced to the person involved and any unusual activities investigated immediately and thoroughly.

Access from remote terminals can pose a threat from unseen, unknown and even undetected intruders, i.e. those people who have come to be known as 'hackers'. Tracing hackers can be very difficult indeed. If you are considering allowing access through the public telephone network, therefore, additional protection should be built in. You can allow access by certain individuals only. You can insist on telephoning the caller back (automatically) and limiting the numbers that can be called to just a few selected ones. Passwords should be changed frequently. There will always be methods of breaching security. Your security system must reflect the value you place on your data and the cost you are prepared to bear.

There is nothing new about companies losing valuable information. Computers just make it easier to lose more, very much more quickly and without anyone being any the wiser. They do, however, provide scope for better protection and so the balance is returned roughly to the status quo. The security of the company's data remains in the hands of its employees. Employee awareness, vigilance and loyalty are the best insurance against losing significant amounts of sensitive information.

- Do not allow casual intruders near your computers.
- Do control access to the system.
- Do not allow anyone to demonstrate or use software of unknown origin on your computers.
- Do maintain a log of access.
- Do make it obvious that you take security very seriously.
- Do ensure that your employees understand the importance of keeping unauthorised people away from the machines.

With regard to safeguarding against loss of data and working time because of system failure, it is possible to set up a system so that it survives all but the most serious disaster. In fact, there are some systems that can reset the system right back to the last keystroke before the disaster. Such systems are fearfully expensive, however. For the small or the small to middle sized business, there are a number of options. Novell has a 'system fault tolerant' version of its operating system. You can run two servers and copy data automatically between them. You can use 'disk mirroring', which automatically guards against one of two hard disks failing, or 'disk duplexing', which guards against both disk failure and disk circuitry failure. Each of these methods bears a significant monetary penalty, but there are slight gains in performance.

14 Extending your system

Splitting the load □ Linking machines together □ Which way to go □ Costings □ Additional discipline □ Complexity

Assume that you started with one stand alone machine and that now, say, after a year's trading, your business is successful and you find that you use your computer for all your correspondence, invoicing, accounts and stock control. At least, you just manage to organise your staff and yourself so that everyone gets enough time on the computer. You now rely on your computer system and, in fact, the business depends upon it.

At this stage in the development of your business, you really should have an in-house fallback position. If something goes wrong you may not be able to work without access to the data for three days and, if demand suddenly increases, you may find yourself working late every day just to keep the accounts and stock control information up to date. You now need to make a decision concerning the second machine.

Splitting the load

One approach would be to get another machine identical to the one you already have, or perhaps the next model up, but certainly 100 per cent compatible with it. You could then do all your word processing on one machine and all the record keeping on the other. If one breaks down, you could simply, with the help of the latest back-up of your data files, revert to the method of working that existed before you introduced the second machine. When the faulty one is repaired you can once again split the work.

Linking machines together

There will come a time when two people will be doing the same type of job, or jobs that complement one another. They will need access to the same computer programs and files. When this happens, it is time to consider some form of multi-user or networking system.

Preparations for this eventuality should really have been taken into account when the stand-alone machine was purchased. It should have been selected with the possible extension to a multi-terminal system in mind. There should be a clear upgrade path from your existing system to the new one. It should not involve learning new applications software. In other words, the software should be available in both single-user and multi-user or networking formats. Clearly, there will be new things to learn about the new system so you do not want to complicate matters by having to learn new applications software at the same time.

Which way to go

There are several options. Whichever you choose, you will be fixing your mode of operation and it will be very expensive to change to an alternative. In particular, your staff will gain experience of one particular system. To substitute a different system at some future date will entail them getting used to its peculiarities and learning new methods of work. They might even need additional training. There will be disruption of routines with consequent loss of efficiency which might not be only temporary. So your choice at this stage has wide implications.

If you chose MSDOS or PCDOS as the operating system for your stand alone machine(s), then it is reasonable for you to continue with something like it. You can do so in a number of ways. For instance, CDOS (Concurrent DOS) allows you to operate a number of terminals from one computer. Alternatively, you can operate in a networking environment, which connects modified stand alone machines to one or more file servers which handle storage, printing and communications for all of them. Another option is to work within the shell of another operating system such as UNIX, which can be specially programmed to handle standard DOS functions. 'Shell' is a computer term used to describe the process whereby, from being in one operating system, you can perform functions of another one. The one described here means that from the Unix operating system you can perform MSDOS activities (i.e. Unix has a DOS shell).

CDOS is an excellent choice for a small system, but there are serious drawbacks if utilisation is heavy and there are more than three or four terminals connected to the master processor. These

14

terminals can be 'dumb' or 'intelligent'. Dumb terminals have no computing power of their own. An intelligent terminal can act as a stand-alone computer, so you can still do *some* computing with PCs if the main machine fails for some reason. With CDOS, however, it would be necessary for an intelligent terminal to work with a special program that makes it function like (or 'emulate') a dumb terminal. So you cannot take advantage of the local processing power when running under CDOS. You rely on just one computer for all computing functions. The master processor needs extra memory to enable it to function efficiently. It will be doing the work of all the terminals and at a certain level of activity it will be fully committed and working without any break. When this happens, terminals have to wait while the master completes processes it has already started. Delays quickly build up and response times become seriously degraded. This limitation will probably never be encountered with two or three terminals and a fast processor; nevertheless, it does exist and its effects can be quite dramatic.

A networking environment that has attained worldwide acceptance is Novell. With this system, terminals use their own local processing power, requesting facilities such as printers and filing functions from one or more 'servers'. The servers take commands from the terminals and respond by reading and writing files or managing printer 'spools' to ensure that requests do not get mixed up. All terminals use the same cable for communications and this can be a serious limitation if the communication rate is not fast enough. A common speed of transmission is about 1.2 million characters per second. This means that the entire memory of most PC type machines can be completely filled in about half a second, so most requests should be dealt with in much less time. With ten terminals and heavy use of the system, all requests should be dealt with in one or two seconds. The bottleneck turns out to be the server. If more servers are added, degradation of performance is less noticeable. This type of system, with one server, is probably the best choice if from four to ten or twelve terminals are needed. The upper limit will depend upon the activity of the terminals. With light average activity and a powerful server, thirty or more terminals can be served perfectly well.

However, it is unlikely that you will be able to use exactly the same programs that you use with your stand alone machine. You will have to upgrade to networking versions that prevent two users from altering the same piece of information in the files at the same time.

On the multi-user front, the UNIX operating system is acclaimed by many as the leader. It has been developed over many years, but there has been a problem with standardisation and software writers have been relatively slow to develop applications for it. There is now a significant body of software available which is perfectly adequate for most data-processing activities. The rapid and widespread acceptance of MSDOS and PCDOS has certainly hampered its progress. It will be perceived as slower in operation than most networks, because communications between terminal and processor are generally slow.

That the terminal-to-processor limitation is common to all multi-user systems should be borne in mind if graphical displays or spreadsheet work is being considered. The local processing power of network terminals enables them to perform such activities at high speed. Another factor of importance is degradation of performance of a multi-user system as additional dumb terminals, each of which uses the power of the central processor, are added. When an intelligent terminal is added to the network, it adds processing power to the system and may only need to call upon the file server occasionally to retrieve or store files. Degradation will, of course, occur on networks when file activity becomes high. The choice between multi-user and networking systems is seldom clear-cut in the small business environment, and, amongst a host of other factors, one must consider the type of work, the loading of the system, the response times required and the support available.

Costings

The cost of a second machine that will not be linked to the first is simple to determine. It will be the cost of the computer plus any additional peripherals required. The same is not true if the two machines are to be linked. There will also be a charge for the new multi-user or network operating system, plus charges for multi-user or networking versions of your software. There is little to choose between the cost of adding a new intelligent terminal to a network and that of a dumb terminal to a multi-user system. You will probably need to have cabling work done. Additional training will be necessary to ensure that the system is operated efficiently. You can expect your maintenance costs to be higher too.

Additional discipline

With the adoption of additional computing facilities, there comes the need for further control over the use of the system(s). If you opt for two stand alone computers and divide the applications between them, then that split must be maintained unless the systems are reconfigured and everyone involved is made aware of the change. Otherwise data can end up on the wrong machine, files can get muddled up and things can become chaotic. Indeed, if you have the same program active on more than one machine, you may be violating the terms of your licence to use the software.

Networks and multi-user systems impose their own discipline to a certain extent, but there remain areas of responsibility that have to be addressed. Someone will have to be trained and take on the designation 'system supervisor'. In a small business this post might be assumed by the proprietor. Ideally, at least two people should be able to look after the system. These people must be trained to recognise when the system is not working properly and must be able to close it down safely, perform routine checks to determine whether maintenance engineers should be called, restart the machine properly and carry out regular activities such as clearing print queues and taking daily back-ups. The jobs are similar to those appropriate to stand alone systems, but they are more complex and the stakes are higher and so a greater level of responsibility is called for.

Complexity

A multi-user or networking environment is very much more complex than a stand alone system. However, it is a natural progression and, if it is what your business requires, you should not be put off. If you have been able to look after your single machine, have imposed the necessary disciplines and been able to understand the principles of operation and appreciate the need for routine activities, then upgrading will not pose any insurmountable obstacles.

Because of the added complexity, you will, of course, choose reputable suppliers with the necessary expertise on hand and with the experience to ensure that your system is installed quickly and efficiently. This is not to say that you do not have the ability to install the system yourself, but there are so many pitfalls that you will almost certainly find yourself spending very much more time on the job than you expected and certainly more time than is good for your business. You should ensure that your suppliers provide sufficient training for you and your staff to be able to look after the system without calling for assistance too frequently.

15 When things go wrong

Problems with hardware □ Problems with software □ How do I put things right? □ Checklist □ Farewell

As with any system, things can go wrong – and they will eventually. You will be able to predict some problems and make preparations to limit the damage. You are entitled to be warned by your supplier of external influences that may cause difficulties and you should receive instruction regarding the recognised way of protecting yourself and restarting your system when conditions allow. Problems internal to your system will be of a different nature. In general, you must take into account five factors – hardware, software, data files, users and methods of working. These factors interact in a highly complex way and you depend upon the skill of the system developer for its smooth functioning.

Problems with hardware

The most obvious feature of a computer system is the hardware. This consists of pieces of man-made machinery each of which has its limitations. Two machines, which appear identical, will have significant differences even if they are made with the same types of components connected together in the same way. This applies, of course, to all machinery – cars, toasters, space shuttles. In the case of computer hardware, some units will be able to work at higher or lower temperatures than others, some will be affected more easily than others by variations in mains voltage and so on. Although we cannot be precise, we know that, eventually, something will go wrong. We try to extend this period of proper functioning as long as possible by treating the equipment with respect, and if it seems to act differently in some circumstances, we can contact the maintenance company for advice.

Since we know that something will eventually go wrong with the hardware, we take measures to minimise the effect of such a failure.

We set up working practices to protect ourselves and design the software to try to detect any abnormalities and to enable us to recover automatically wherever economically feasible.

Another kind of hardware fault is one that has entered at the design stage and not been revealed by tests. Conflicts between various components in unusual circumstances have come to light on some machines many months after they have been released onto the market. Such faults are very rare and it would take an expert to recognise one.

Problems with software

Applications software is designed to perform a particular task for the enterprise. An accounting package should produce details of the business's financial condition. (This was not true in the early days of microcomputers when the market was flooded with a great deal of totally inadequate software.) These days, however, you can be pretty certain that it will work reasonably well. But this assumes that the rest of the system is functioning properly – that the working methods are being followed correctly, the users are not making mistakes, the data files are not corrupted and that the hardware has no faults. Gross error in the design of software is now rare and the designers of the software would normally be only too keen to correct any faults that do come to light.

Your data files, which change in response to the entry of new data, are the most vulnerable and most valuable part of your system. You can go out and buy new hardware and software, you can hire new people and you can define new working practices, but your data files are yours alone. Nobody else has (or should have) your data. This is the reason that so much emphasis is placed on protecting your files and on taking regular back-up copies. If they become corrupted, then it may be impossible to recover completely. There is but one way of protecting your investment and that is to take copies and store them safely where they cannot be stolen, where they cannot be destroyed, for instance by fire, and where they will not be subjected to strong magnetic fields. Taking back-up copies of your data files is probably the most important activity of each day.

It is on record that an accounting software package was installed in a solicitors' office by a company that did not inform the users that back-up copies should be made. The system worked flawlessly for three years and then it gradually began to go wrong and finally the accounts were found to be in complete disarray. The solicitor successfully sued the company for failing in its duty to ensure that the accounts were properly backed up. The company had to pay a five figure sum in compensation.

How do I put things right?

Your first port of call when things go wrong soon after installation, and when the system is still under warranty, will be your suppliers. It is their responsibility to make sure that what they recommended and supplied to you keeps working to specification. However, some things may be beyond their control, and provided they are making their best endeavours to get your system up and working, then they will have discharged their duty. Most suppliers will carry out their responsibilities reasonably well because it is not in their best interests to become known for poor and inadequate service. Warranty repairs usually mean that you have to wait while your supplier sends the equipment back to the manufacturer for servicing, and this may take up to ten or fifteen days. Much longer than this may mean that you have a case for reimbursement.

After the warranty period, you will have to rely on someone to carry out repairs and maintenance for you. A local supplier with in-house maintenance support or a local computer maintenance company will usually be satisfactory, as will the national networks that have been set up by the larger manufacturers. However, if these people take excessively long to complete their work, or if the system continually fails to work properly for a variety of reasons, you may again have recourse to the maintenance company. As recommended in an earlier chapter, it is a good idea to maintain a log of system operations, noting down the activities on your machine each day. It need not be anything elaborate. When your system goes wrong, you should note down the calls made to the maintenance company, the ways in which you get around the problem, the time it takes for the company to respond, and sufficient information to give some idea of the cost of doing the work without the computer system. If the maintenance company seems incapable of ever getting your system going, you may be able to seek compensation through the courts, but before you consider going down this route you must, of course, seek legal advice.

If you have gone out and bought different parts of your computer system from different suppliers, then you will find it very difficult to place the blame for any problems you encounter. A computer system can be extremely complex and it is often very difficult to determine the cause of many faults. The hardware supplier will blame the software supplier and vice versa when the cause might be the

15

way the networking system has been installed. An example of such a situation arose at one installation when it appeared that the hard disk drive was giving trouble. From time to time the files of an accounting package became corrupt. As the hard disk filled up so the problem became progressively more severe. It was not until the accounting files were carefully examined that it was discovered that chunks of word processing documents were appearing in them. It turned out that there was a bug in an early version of a multi-tasking operating system, which allowed the word processor to overwrite accounts files. As a footnote, the business managed to carry on with its work in spite of this problem because it was very careful always to take and preserve back-up copies.

It is far better to get everything from one source and require a guarantee of compatibility amongst the components. You then have just one company, and ultimately one person, the managing director, to deal with. If you have difficulty getting satisfaction from a company, you should set out, in writing, the history of your problems and the contacts you have had with the company. These should be incorporated in a letter to the MD, written in unemotional terms, containing nothing that can be taken as hostile, but simply asking for the situation to be resolved quickly. You will almost certainly get the results you are looking for. After all, the MD is your counterpart in the other company and if you found out that your company was failing in some respect, you would want to put it right as quickly as possible.

Checklist

To summarise these ideas, the following list offers tips on minimising problems and getting them solved when they occur:

- Buy from one supplier or through one agent.
- Make sure that the equipment is compatible.
- Foster good relations with the supplier.
- Make regular back-ups and keep them secure.
- Log all non-trivial problems and report them immediately.
- Try to get cooperation when things start to go wrong.

Go down the legal route only when all other avenues have been exhausted and then claim for every expense incurred as a result of the problems you have been having.

Farewell

We very much hope that this book has gone some way to pointing out some of the obstacles that might confront you, and setting you on the right tracks towards the whole process of computerisation.

If carried out in the right way, computerisation can be extremely profitable and an enjoyable experience.

Our concluding chapter is a case study of how a small and expanding motor firm went about the process of installing and implementing a computer system. The case study is designed to help consolidate your knowledge of computerisation and demonstrate good practice.

16 A final case study

This case study is based on an imaginary private limited company that specialises in both the hiring of motor vehicles and their repair and maintenance.

The company decided to investigate the possibility of employing the use of a computer to carry out much of its data processing activities. After many hours of deliberation between the three directors who own the company, a letter was drafted and sent to five vendors, all of whom were local. It read:

To: Pitcraft Motor Repairs & Hire Co. Ltd,
                       20 The Hyde,
                       London W2

                       5 September 199X

Re: Business Computer System

Dear Sirs,

We write to you as prospective suppliers of our new business computer system in the hope that you will be able to supply us with a quote and proposal for such a new computer system.
   Our business has two main activities:

1. Renting motor vehicles. We have a fleet of twenty cars and six trucks which are rented to customers on a flexible basis.
2. Servicing and repair of vehicles.

   We are a private limited company managed and run by three directors. We have been trading for eighteen years and have steadily grown in size over these years. Our growth is such that we are hoping to purchase additional premises two miles away from our current site. The new site will be our new repair and maintenance site while our existing site will concentrate on the hiring and will be our administration headquarters.
   Our customers who hire cars vary quite considerably, but are chiefly private individuals with, occasionally, companies looking for cars and trucks to help them at their peak times. On average, 70 per cent of our vehicles are rented out at any one time.
   On the repair side, much of our mechanics' time is spent:

1. Servicing our own fleet of cars.
2. Servicing cars for their MOT.
3. Carrying out daily repairs, such as tyre and exhaust refits, and general repairs.

The company presently employs four motor mechanics, two administration staff and one supervisor. In addition to this, I and one of my co-directors are actively involved managing the business, with the other director only occasionally getting involved.

We have very few suppliers. They are mainly the two motor manufacturers who supply our car fleet. On occasion we have to use other suppliers, who are found when needed.

With the growth in business activity, the amount of paper work required and the establishment of a new site, we feel the time has now come to employ a computer system to handle a lot of our administration. The duties of the two administration staff include:

1. Running a booking system for car maintenance and MOT tests for both our own fleet and for customers. It is important that when a customer requests a booking we are able to give an answer straight away. In practice, if a customer cannot get an immediate response they will go elsewhere.
2. Running a booking system for the leasing of cars. The need for immediate response is exactly the same as that for maintenance.
3. Invoicing our customers. Up to twenty invoices need producing daily. When invoicing our customers for car hire, it is important that mileage and dates are strictly monitored. One of our problems recently has been chasing up customers who have hired cars in the past. We need to access this kind of information for the occasional police inquiry and for passing on parking fines to the people responsible.
4. The selling of cars is a fairly standard accounting exercise, although details of cars sold and purchased by our company have to be maintained on records for a long time. Selling is very limited as we only sell former fleet cars.
5. Purchasing is a specialist job which requires market research and constant appraisal of where we buy from. Such purchasing will involve new cars for our fleet as well as spare parts and accessories. Although we require good record handling from a computer, it is difficult for us to see how a computer can be of much help in making buying decisions.

16

We feel that our immediate requirement for a computer is to meet the needs of the booking system. The system must allow our administration staff to respond to a customer immediately an inquiry or booking is made. It is also important that the maintenance site of our business can access the booking information on repairs and be able to make some bookings, and alterations to bookings themselves. We would hope, therefore, that a computer can print work schedules out regularly and alert relevant people about alterations. With both booking systems, we would need to be able to make alterations quickly and efficiently.

The selling and buying parts of the business activity of the firm require no urgent action as they do not generate too much administration work and, within reason, such administration can be carried out during slack periods of the working day.

Some word processing capabilities would be very useful because this might enable us to do far more marketing of our services.

As directors we have never really handled computers before and so have no preferences for any particular system.

Both of our administration staff have gained some experience of computers in word processing and simple accounts from college and schools they have attended in the past. Training, however, will be essential in order to cope with a new system. Training needs should be extended to all staff in the firm, although we would not expect all staff to receive exactly the same kind of training.

Our budget for computing is limited to £25,000 for immediate expenditure. We would like an estimate in any proposal as to what the running costs of such a system would be for the first two years. We would also like a quote to include on-site maintenance for at least one year.

We look forward to hearing from you in due course about a new computer system. If we have not heard from you six weeks after the date of this letter, we shall assume you are unable to offer us a quote.

Yours faithfully

Director

Within two weeks of sending these letters, two vendors got in contact and arranged visits to the firm. One other vendor responded shortly after by returning a written quote and details of a proposed system.

The first vendor's representative spent a good deal of time questioning the directors about their methods of doing things and the kind of time scales they were anticipating when setting up and running the new site. The representative clearly showed a good deal of understanding about the kinds of problems the business faced and even informed the directors about his own experience on the kind of business expansion they were about to undergo. He said their computing needs would best be served by a local area network at the administration site of the business allowing up to three users to work with the computer at the same time. Meanwhile, the new site would have its own computer with a telephone link between this computer and the administration centre, giving the same access to the network as any other machine.

The second vendor's representative asked many technical questions and then started on a fairly 'hard' sales talk on the hardware and software that the firm needed. Because he used a good deal of technical jargon, it was difficult to understand what the business would end up with based purely on this visit.

Of the three written quotes that eventually came in, the company immediately abandoned the quote from the firm who made the latter visit. This was because it was well over budget and left out from the quote the maintenance costs and projected running costs which had been requested.

From the two quotes to choose from, the firm eventually went for the one whose representative had impressed them so much. Although both quotes were within budget and fairly comprehensive in coverage, the deciding factors were:

---

1. **The knowledge and experience demonstrated by the representative showed clear understanding of the problems such a business faces. It was felt that this would be reflected in the kind of computer solution implemented.**
2. **After telephone dialogue with the vendors, the chosen vendor had given an assurance that staff training would be given on-site at the required times.**
3. **The track record of the vendor was better in the business area in question and with respect to financial soundness.**

With respect to both software and hardware chosen, there was very little difference. The company read this to mean that the best solution available within the budget set down had probably been selected by both firms.

The selected firm promptly installed the new network system at the administration centre and spent two days installing the software and testing the system.

Another two days were spent training staff in how to use the

16

booking system on the computer. They began by building up a database of all outstanding bookings and practised cancelling bookings, creating bookings and making a whole series of amendments to bookings. After just five weeks from installation, the booking system was implemented.

Over the next month the following developments occurred:

- The actual booking system from an operator's point of view had become well established and was regarded as fairly easy to operate.
- A system of backing up data had been implemented and was part of the daily routine of operations.
- A management information system had been implemented where managers could extract a whole series of reports on car availability and repairs, and could interrogate the computer on usage of particular cars at any point in time, and so on.

During this operation, the maintenance side of the business was moved to another site. The contracted firm placed a computer at this site and modems at both sites to allow the required link-up. Some staff training was conducted at the new site to allow mechanics to extract job lists, bookings and special details or instructions regarding any given job. Again, this went reasonably well although adjustments had to be made to the equipment to improve the telephone link between the sites.

The company carried on with the system for three months. During this period, someone was called out to make repairs to the system on four occasions. Although the company had a maintenance contract to cover such instances, one of the failures did cause a few problems. As a result of the computer being 'down', the company resolved to establish a back-up system quickly in case this ever happened again.

The third stage was implemented after five months of operation: the installation of the accounts system. The accounts system was software developed by the firm who produced the booking system. Consequently, operators found no problem in understanding how to use the package. Two staff and one director were sent on a short course in order to learn the package, but found this of little real benefit. All staff learnt how to use the package effectively by trial and error and thinking very carefully about how they would organise accounts. For example, one of the effects of computerisation was to establish a daily slot where invoices and customer payments would be processed rather than attempt to enter details as the transactions occurred. This establishment of a whole set of procedures took a good deal of time, but was something that was regarded as long overdue irrespective of whether they had computerised or not. In fact, after the new computerised system had settled, the firm began to review a whole set of procedures in order to improve the flow of data processing and the relevance of the information that could be extracted from the computer.

The company was now in a position where any further development could be carried out with a good deal of confidence and the directors all felt that they could cope with these developments more independently and without so much outside help.

The company, for example, implemented both spreadsheets and word processing on their computer system using the skills of the operators rather than training agencies or consultants.

16

Appendix 1: Glossary of computing terms

Abort. Stopping the execution of a program while it is still running. If you are in the middle of, say, updating a record, you may need to abort it to avoid a serious error. In most packages this is usually done by hitting the Esc key. Switching the machine off while a program is running will also abort the program but should never be done as this will probably cause loss of data.

Access. The activity of referring to data stored in a file. For example, disk access is needed if a sales ledger activity is going to keep customer records updated.

Analyst. A person who has the job of analysing various activities, such as a systems analyst, database analyst, cost analyst. Systems analysts are often concerned with analysing computer based information systems or manual systems with a view to computerising them.

Application. A specific use to which a computer is put, e.g. payroll, word processing, job costing. Such applications are often performed on a computer by a software package, or part of an integrated software package.

Audit trail. The term has many meanings, chief among them being recording a sequence of transactions in such a way that any transaction can be traced back. Audit trails can take the form of printed transactions lists or transactions files. Audit trails are required to allow auditors to check accounts, or personnel to track errors or restore to a computer database lost transactions data.

Background printing. A process where the computer prints a document and at the same time allows an operator to go on using the computer to process data.

Backing storage. Often referred to as secondary storage, this allows data to be stored on media such as disks for long term purposes; i.e. off-line data storage.

Back-up. A process of copying all data from one source to another for safekeeping, e.g. from a hard disk to either floppy disks or tape.

Bar code. Often found on retail products, the bar code is a set of printed vertical bars that holds information about the product, such as where it was made, who made it, weight or size. Computers are able to read them quickly using a bar code reader. Such details can, for example, enable computers to determine a price for the product by accessing a related record in a database.

Batch processing. The process of grouping transactions together and then processing them all in one go. For example, a firm may choose to enter all invoice details sent to it by suppliers at predefined times in the week, rather than entering them up as and when they arrive.

Bootstrap. A small program built into the computer that instructs the system about how to set itself up when switched on. Part of the bootstrap is often held on disk, which is also needed when the machine is switched on.

Buffer. A part of memory used as a temporary store to hold data from an input device. For example, most printers have a buffer memory for storing data prior to printing it. Also keyboards often hold at least one line of data before it is sent to the computer's processor.

Bug. An error in a program.

Bus. A type of communication channel which data travels along. Such communication channels consist of a control bus, data bus, address bus and peripheral bus.

Byte. A measure of computer memory, normally containing eight single bits. Each byte often represents a single character. 1,024 of these bytes are referred to as a kilobyte.

Carriage return. A single character sent to the computer by pressing the RETURN key on the keyboard. Such carriage returns are often used to release data from the keyboard buffer to the computer's processor.

Character. A single element in coded form for the processor, such as a letter or a single-number digit. Such characters are normally represented by eight bits, or one byte.

Clock. A processor contains an electronic pulse generator that is used to transmit synchronised pulses to different parts of the computer for the interpretation and execution of instructions. Such synchronisation will be set at a speed that determines the computer's *clock speed*. Clock speeds are measured in megahertz (MHz). The faster the clock speed, the greater the internal processing speed of the computer. For most business applications, it is the access time to disks, rather than the clock speed, that is important to processing speed.

Command. An instruction to the computer to perform a given task.

Computer aided design (CAD). The use of a computer with graphics software to design through electronic drawing. Main applications areas are in the fields of engineering drawing, product design, fashion design and technical drawing.

Computer bureau. A commercial enterprise offering computing services to organisations. Many firms still use computer bureaux to manage their payrolls. Some computer bureaux can offer on-line services by installing a terminal at the firm and thereby offering computing time on a time sharing basis.

Corruption. A term used to refer to the loss, or corruption, of data. Data corruption is a particular problem when it occurs on a disk. Such corruption can often render data on a disk useless; hence the importance of regular backing-up of data.

Cursor. A small image such as a block or dash on the screen to indicate where data will be entered from the keyboard.

Daisy wheel printer. A type of impact printer that prints characters by striking the character images on carbonated ribbon. The characters appear at the end of spokes on a small wheel. The characters on paper are of a high quality although the print style is limited to the characters on the wheel. They are particularly good for letter or report writing.

Data. An element that will need processing to form the basis of information. Data can take the form of an electronic pulse, a magnetic particle, a hole in a piece of paper, a particle of light or any other physical form that can be represented in one of two states. It is the pattern of this data that will be interpreted and processed by the computer.

Database. The collection, in a structured form, of all data that represents the basis of information for an organisation's business applications. Most business applications are forms of pre-structured databases, although database packages exist on the market whereby users can determine exactly how data is to be structured.

Data capture. The way in which data is captured, collected or input for processing. Methods of data capture can vary from entering data by bar code readers reading bar codes, scanners, optical character recognition, source documents requiring keying in. The methods of direct input to the computer are increasing, as data capture is often the most time consuming and error prone part of general data processing operations.

App 1

Datel. The Post Office data transmission facility available to commerce and industry. It allows the transmission of data between points on either private or public telephone lines. Datel offers a wide and varied service to meet the needs of differing data communication systems.

Dedicated computer. A computer system set up to perform one specific task or set of tasks. For example, a cash dispenser or an electronic cash till.

Default. When offering a choice to users through software, a default value is assumed if no choice is made.

Deletion. The process of removing data from a system, such as a customer record or transaction.

Diagnostic routine. A program used to detect errors in either software or hardware. Many diagnostic routines will operate in a way that does not interfere with normal operations and is not apparent to a user.

Disk drive. A peripheral device for storing data generated by the computer's processor and for retrieving data by the processor. Disk drives can contain either floppy disks or hard disks.

DOS (disk operating system). Part of the software that is contained on disk, is loaded into computer memory and is used to operate the computer system.

Download. The process of loading a program into computer memory.

Down time. The amount of time a computer is not functioning.

Driver. A part of the operating system software that is used to control certain peripheral devices. Computers will need disk drivers, screen drivers and so on.

Duplex. A communications concept that allows simultaneous data transmission down a line in both directions.

EFTPOS (electronic funds transfer at point of sale). This allows funds to be transferred from a customer's account to a trader's account as and when a transaction takes place, thereby avoiding cash transfer.

Electronic mail. A process of transmitting messages between computers electronically. Such mail can be stored for future reference.

EPOS (electronic point of sale). A device such as in check-out systems in supermarkets that can scan bar codes and price the products.

Exception reporting. A process of reporting any circumstances that are unusual or not normally permitted, such as large customer orders or low stock levels.

Expert system. Software orientated, an expert system enables a computer to diagnose problems, given the symptoms. Expert systems often contain information about past events and calculate likely causes of problems through statistical analysis.

Fibre optics. A cabling medium for transmitting data; an alternative form to coaxial cable. It transmits data via light pulses and allows much greater speed and reliable capacity than coaxial cable.

Field. An element of a record that is a collection of characters such as that which makes up a customer name or stock number.

File. A collection of records that are related in some way. A stock file, for example, may be a collection of stock records.

File protection. A method of protecting files from corruption or accidental erasure. A common way of protecting a file is to write protect it, which means the file can be read but not written to.

File server. A storage device that is shared by a number of microcomputers on a local area network. Such networks can have more than one file server; they are used to store information that all computers can access and they enable the sharing of other resources, such as printers.

Floppy disk. A backing store medium used to store data. Floppy disks require a disk drive in order for the computer to both read from them and write to them.

Format. The way data is structured on disk, paper or screens. With respect to disks, it is important that new disks are formatted in a way that is compatible with the computer system before they are used. Disk formatting from your own machine will ensure compatibility.

Form feed. A process whereby a sheet of paper is fed through a printer. The process is often used to align continuous paper on a printer to the top of the next sheet.

Function. A general term used to identify a specific group of related tasks, such as the accounting function, stock control function or payroll function.

General purpose computer. A computer that can be adapted to a wide range of applications by loading the appropriate software.

Generation of files. A process based on the grandfather-father-son principle for creating age categories of backed-up files. With the cost of storage being relatively low, it is often prudent to keep many generations of backed-up files.

Hacking. A term used for the act of trying to gain unauthorised access to computerised information, such as trying to use modem equipment to gain access to private information held on computer databases.

Handshaking. A process where computer and peripheral tell each other that data transmission is ready to commence. A printer requires this because it is normally unable to print data as fast as it can receive it, so the principle of handshaking ensures data is sent down as and when the printer is ready, thereby preventing loss.

Hard copy. Printed output from a computer.

Hardware. The physical attributes of any computer system.

Housekeeping. The practice of keeping track of what information is stored on disks and tapes. Good housekeeping will prevent disks from becoming cluttered, speed up processing and lessen the chance of filling up a disk unnecessarily.

Icon. A pictorial representation of programs, document files and options available for executing or processing. Icons are often used as an alternative to text menus and directories and are typical of the windows software that is often distributed with new machines.

Image processing. A process of transmitting, in digitised form, pictures and images. This is often the technique used to get pictures into a document produced by a desk top publishing application.

Impact printers. A category of printer that creates images on paper by physically hitting the paper, such as matrix or daisy wheel printers.

Interface. A general term used to describe the processing of data between two systems or sub-systems. For example, a disk interface refers to the process of transferring data from processor to disk and back. Such interfaces are collections of both hardware and software.

Job. In a computing context, this refers to either routines or applications being run on a computer system at any one point in time.

Keyboard. One of the most used forms of input devices.

Key field. A field within a record that identifies the record itself and is used to access the record.

Kilobyte (kbyte). Used to measure data quantity, a kilobyte represents 1,024 bytes of data.

Kimball tag. Either pre-punched or magnetised card containing information about an item. Often seen in retail outlets, kimball tags are used as a storage medium that can hold details about a product. An appropriate computer input device can then read them.

Laser printer. A type of non-impact printer giving high quality printed output. Its technology is based on similar techniques to those of photocopiers.

Line printer. Low quality, very high speed printers that print complete lines at a time. These are not the kind of printers you would associate with a small business machine or network. They are more common in the big financial institutions such as banks and local authorities. They are normally driven by mini or mainframe computer systems.

Local area network (LAN). A system that connects a number of microcomputers so that they can share common resources such as a database or printer. While resources can be shared, each computer on a network is still able to act independently of the others.

Logging in. A method of getting access to a computer's information. Designed for security, the process of logging in requires an operator to enter identification and, normally, an associated password. It is of particular use on networks or integrated software packages where operators can be limited in what software and information they can access.

Logging out. Signing off a system; an activity that should be carried out whenever an operator has finished work on a computer network.

Magnetic disk. A storage medium for data which fits into a disk drive. There are many different types of disk, suitable for different types of application and computer systems.

Magnetic ink character recognition (MICR). Typically used by the banks, magnetic ink characters are read by the computer as a way of inputting data to the computer. Magnetic characters typically appear at the bottom of cheques and are used to assist banks in processing a large volume of cheques.

Magnetic tape. A form of backing store medium that is mounted onto tape drives or into tape streamers to store, serially, data. Magnetic tapes offer an effective and cheap form of back-up storage for systems with a large amount of data. They are also used for storing programs that are subsequently loaded into computer memory.

Mainframe computer. An exceptionally large computer often capable of supporting many hundreds of computer terminals, microcomputers, storage units, printers and other peripherals. Quite often mainframe computers are used as a large central processor supporting remote systems by data communication links across long distances.

Management information system (MIS). Often used in conjunction with other data processing activities, MIS is used to extract a whole series of reports. With most MIS packages, users are able to identify their own information needs and extract reports to meet these.

Matrix printer. An impact printer that creates an image on paper through a dot pattern on a matrix. Such matrix printers are effective for printing, at low cost, graphics as well as near letter quality text. These printers are normally adequate for most small business applications.

Microprocessor. The more common description of the processing unit of a microcomputer.

Minicomputer. Similar to a mainframe computer but on a smaller scale. The distinction between a mainframe computer and a minicomputer is not an obvious one, but minicomputers are often multi-user/tasking machines that can support many peripherals (about 100) on both a local and distributed processing basis.

Modulator/demodulator (modem). A device for both sending and receiving signals down a telephone line, thereby allowing data communication between computer devices. Modems are needed at both ends of a line to allow data communications to work.

Module. A function within a program package that can often be used in isolation from other modules. For example, in the Pegasus system there is a Sales Ledger module, Purchase Ledger module, Nominal Ledger module and so on.

Multiplexor. A communications device that receives data from a number of computer devices and then sends it down *one* telephone line. There will be a slowing down in data transmission from each device as more multiplexers transmit data, but such devices can reduce the costs of data communications quite considerably.

Off-line. A general term referring to data or part of a computer system being inaccessible. For instance, data on a disk which is not in the computer disk drive is said to be off-line.

Off-line data processing. A process of working on data away from the main computer system or on, say, a microcomputer before interacting with the main system. With the cost and power of microcomputers, it often makes sense to prepare data, such as invoices, off-line and then batch process the work on a mainframe computer or minicomputer later. Off-line processing can involve many manual operations, e.g. preparation and validation of data, before computerised (on-line) processing.

Operating system. Software that is used to operate the computer and its peripherals.

Operator. A term used to describe a person who operates a computer. This is different from a person who programs a computer, a computer programmer.

Optical character reader (OCR). A computer input device that recognises characters, usually in typed form. An OCR can save a considerable amount of labour when text that has already been typed needs to be entered to the computer.

Parallel running. A process of running two systems together: typically a computer system and a manual system. This may be a necessary prerequisite to automating a manual process with computers. Such parallel processing will help to detect any errors or bugs in the new system. Eventually, such parallel running will have to end.

Password. A way of ensuring that only authorised personnel have access to parts of a system. Passwords are only effective if they are kept secret from everyone except authorised persons. Passwords are also set up in a way that ensures different people have access to different parts of the system.

Peripheral device. Input, output and storage device of a computer that constitutes part of a system's hardware.

POS. Point of sale.

Prestel. A public database service offered by British Telecom.

Protocol. Communications protocol is a standard of data communications that tries to ensure compatibility in the way data is communicated across lines.

Random file. A file organisation principle that allows the computer to directly access any record without having to read all records preceding it sequentially. Naturally, such files are normally stored on disk medium.

Read/write heads. A device contained within a disk drive or tape drive that either reads data into the computer or writes data onto the storage medium from the computer.

Real-time processing. A concept of ensuring files and databases are updated by transactions as the transactions occur. To achieve real-time processing, procedure on operating a computer system is just as important as having the hardware and software capabilities to do it.

Remote job entry (RJE). The process of entering data to a computer where the entry point is geographically separate from the main computer system. RJE is typified by a remote computer being linked by modem to a file server.

Report generator. A part of a software package that allows users to design their own reports based on their information needs. It allows considerable freedom in the way users can extract from the system available data. Most accounting packages now offer this software facility.

ROM (read-only memory). A part of the memory in a computer used to store programs in a permanent way. Part of a computer's operating system (e.g. BIOS) is stored on ROM. Some systems will also have applications software built into ROM.

App

Run. The actual execution of a program.

Scheduling. A process of determining the order in which jobs are performed or executed. Such activities can be done automatically or by operating, with priorities being set on certain jobs. Scheduling is required on file servers when users on different machines want both printing and file access work done.

Scrolling. A process of running text up the screen when you want to view data past the bottom of the screen. The alternative to scrolling is to clear the screen then view the contents of one screen at a time.

Silicon chip. A small piece of silicon based material used to hold computer circuits to form a microprocessor. New technology has allowed many thousands of transistors and diodes to be stored on one single chip.

Soft copy. A term used for screen output.

Software. All computer programs from operating system to applications software.

Sort. A data processing term used when rearranging files into a different order.

Spool. Often referred to as a file awaiting printing. On a network, you may be using a central printer along with other users. By spooling files, the actual printing is carried out when the printer is ready. It ensures that no muddles occur by two or more files being printed simultaneously.

Stand alone system. A computer that is capable of working in isolation from any other system. Most microcomputers are stand alone systems.

Storage capacity. The amount of data that can be stored. Storage capacity is normally measured in kilobytes.

Suite. A set of interrelated programs. A term often used instead of package.

Systems analysis. The job of analysing systems, both manual and computerised, with a view to implementing new systems or modifying existing ones. The job of a systems analyst will often include implementing systems, a role that requires communications and business management skills as much as computing ones.

Telecommunications. Refers to the general concept of sending data from one device to another down a telephone line.

Teleprocessing. The use of telecommunications in order to achieve on-line data processing. In other words, to interact with a database from a distance using transmission lines and a terminal.

Telex. As part of British Telecom's Datel service, telex is used for transmitting text only, from one terminal to another, producing printed output at the receiving end.

Test data. Data generated and specifically used for testing systems and their software. Often, copies of live data form a useful set of test data. However, test data may have to be created when being used to test a new system or set of software.

Time sharing. A technique where a processor shares its time among two or more users. Some operating systems have time sharing built in. File servers for networks also need time sharing capabilities in order to support users' demands.

Transaction data. Any data generated from the result of a transaction such as a sale or purchase or stock movement. Transaction data will often be stored as a record per transaction in a set of transaction files and will be used to update master files.

Turnkey system. A system for simply switching on and starting. Turnkey systems are normally supplied by outside agencies or consultancy services. Everything has been installed specifically for the business.

User friendly. A term often associated with the way software guides a user through processes when using a computer application package.

Utility program. A program that can be used to manage files or perform activities outside the normal scope of running a program, such as file back-up, retrieving lost files and deleting unwanted files.

Validation. A process of checking whether data conforms to expected input such as valid date, or ensuring that alphabetic characters are not entered when the computer expects a number.

Verification. A way of confirming with an operator that data input is complete and correct or a certain action is what is required. The 'ARE YOU SURE' message typifies this.

Visual display unit (VDU). The screen that displays text and graphic output as soft copy.

Winchester drive. A storage device that holds a hard disk. The hard disk is non-removable but offers high storage density and capacity and is generally very reliable.

Window. A method of sectioning the VDU in such a way that an operator can see different parts of a document or run different applications at the same time.

Word processing. An application that involves processing words and spending time perfecting format, spelling and so on before producing hard copy. Word processors are replacing typewriters at a growing rate.

App 1

Xenix. An operating system associated with large multi-user and networked microcomputers. The operating system is a standard that is used on many different models of machines and is not associated with one particular manufacturer.

Appendix 2:   An outline of the Data Protection Act

The Data Protection Act of 1984 is concerned with personal information that has been stored on computers. The Act has given basic rights to those individuals on whom the information is held, and places certain obligations on businesses.

If your business holds information about individual people on a computer, then the Act may affect you. Under the Act there are certain obligations:

1. **To register with the Data Protection Registrar.**
2. **To maintain certain good practices regarding such data.**
3. **To allow access to such information to those people on whom you hold data.**

In many respects, if you follow the guidelines we suggest, the implications of this Act for your business should be nil.

Registration

Only those businesses using personal data on individuals should consider registering. The Act calls such individuals *data subjects*. If you use the information on data subjects for anything other than strict accounting purposes, then you will be required to register this information with the Registrar.

For example, if you use customer details for market analysis and mail shot purposes then you should register. On the other hand, if the information is simply used for running the sales ledger, such as sending invoices and statements, then you may be exempt from registering.

Once you have registered, the information you have lodged with the Registrar becomes available to any member of the public on request.

If you do need to register under the Act, you will be referred to as the *data user*. The process of registering involves filling in two forms which are available from main post offices, and posting them to the Registrar's office with a registration fee. At the time of writing the fee is £22. The forms require the following information:

- *Form A*. Details about the location of your company and how either the Registrar's office or members of the public can make contact with the firm.
- *Form B*. The nature of data held about data subjects and the purpose for which it is held.

If you are unable to obtain the forms from a post office, then apply direct to the Registrar's Office:

> The Office of the Data Protection Registrar,
> Springfield House,
> Water Lane,
> Wilmslow, Cheshire SK9 5AX.

If you are in doubt about whether or not you should register, either seek advice or go ahead and register.

If at some time in the future the nature of data held, or what you want to use it for, changes, then you are obliged to register again.

Registration only lasts three years, after which time you will have to register again.

Maintain good practices

Once registered under the Act, a business has a legal duty to abide by some principles relating to personal data, though we would hope that these principles are adopted for all data held on a computer at all times.

- The data collected and processed must have been lawfully and fairly obtained.
- The data can only be used for lawful purposes.
- The data held on individuals is only held for the purposes quoted when you registered.
- The data can only be disclosed to registered recipients.
- The data should be adequate and relevant to the user.
- The data should be accurate and up to date.
- The data should be held for no longer than is necessary.
- Appropriate security of data should be enforced.

- The data should be made available to data subjects on request:

    (a) without being updated or altered or tampered with,
    (b) in a form that can be read.

Rights of data subjects

On this last point, you can charge data subjects a fee providing it covers your costs only. When a request is made by a data subject for information on them, then *all* data about them must be revealed and supplied within forty days of the request. You should ask for reasonable identification before disclosure.

If you do hold personal data about individuals, then make sure that extracting information about individuals is:

- Complete.
- Easily accessible for your own benefit.
- Does not incur heavy costs; you are not allowed to pass on unreasonable costs to a data subject.

App 2

Appendix 3: Sources of information

Publications

There are a large number of publications on the market where information on business computing can be sought and where computer suppliers advertise quite extensively. These publications are available at most large stationers and newsagents, and they fall into a number of categories:

1. Business computing magazines are written for the user who is in business, and normally contain details of latest hardware and software developments as well as articles on topical issues. Some magazines of this type are:

   Computer Express
   Computer Shopper
   Computer Weekly
   PC Plus
   Personal Computer World
   Which Computer?
   Which PC?

   For a business that has established itself well with a computer system, this kind of publication can be very useful and informative. .
2. System related magazines are tailored for a specific make of machine. If there is such a magazine for the system you have, then be careful that it is not written solely for the technical expert or games enthusiast.
3. Technical magazines are really for the computer enthusiast or electronics expert.
4. Games magazines.

Many magazines give away disks containing free software. Such software is either relatively small and cheap, or a distribution disk marketing software. Such disks can help you to become acquainted with software products on the market, or can be formatted for your machine and employed for a more useful purpose.

Training providers

Providers of training exist in most areas in the country and details can normally be found in the *Yellow Pages*. Training providers fall into a number of broad categories:

1. Training companies or subsidiaries of software firms have been established all around the country with the sole purpose of providing training for business users. Most of these training firms can offer on-site training as well as training at their own centres.
2. Most areas in the UK have established information technology centres (ITECs) for the specific purpose of training in the field of information technology. Apart from being a useful source of training, as they train school leavers they can be a place to recruit newly trained staff.
3. Local colleges and polytechnics may well offer both consultancy and training and are worth contacting.

Appendix 4: A brief guide to using MSDOS

What is MSDOS?

MSDOS stands for MicroSoft Disk Operating System and is an operating system most commonly supplied with microcomputers. MSDOS is normally stored on a disk and is loaded in the computer's RAM when needed.

A part of the operating system is loaded into computer memory when the machine is activated and it programs the computer to recognise such commands as 'DIR' and 'CHDIR'. The rest of the operating system is left on disk until required. That part of the operating system loaded at boot-up is normally held in a file called 'COMMAND.COM' while the rest of MSDOS will be a collection file used when required such as 'FORMAT' and 'BACKUP'.

MSDOS allows the user to make use of the computer in a way that does not require vast knowledge of computer electronics or of how the machine has been put together. It allows, through commands, the following:

- Obtaining a listing (directory) of what is held on disks. Computer data will be grouped into files and it is information about what files you have on a disk and some of their characteristics that can be useful when managing computer data.
- Copying files from one place to another. Especially important when backing up files or transferring them between machines.
- Renaming or deleting files.
- Setting the internal clock.
- Running programs stored on disk.
- Creating and organising directories. MSDOS manages files on disks in a directory structure, which will be outlined later in this appendix.

When you first switch on and your system has booted up, you should see displayed on your screen a *system prompt* such as:

A>

Some systems may well be set up to do something different on boot-up or show a different prompt. However, when your machine displays such a prompt it is awaiting a system command. The following list is a sample of the commands that can be entered from this prompt and you should refer to your system manual for a fuller explanation and a more complete list of commands.

Directories and listings

DIR simply lists the contents that are held in a directory on your disk, e.g.

```
Volume in drive C is BUSINESS
Directory of C: \

AUTOEXEC BAT        128    17-09-89   12:12
CONFIG     SYS      128    17-02-88   20:11
COMMAND    COM    23612    15-05-87   12:00
SYS        COM     4607    15-05-87   12:00
123            <DIR>        6-04-90   20:10
COBOL          <DIR>        4-12-89   16:15
DBASE3         <DIR>        4-01-90   18:36
MSDOS          <DIR>       22-12-89    8:46
PASCAL         <DIR>        4-01-90   17:35
SAGE           <DIR>       30-06-89   17:21
SIDEKICK       <DIR>       16-05-89   15:49
WP             <DIR>       21-12-89   19:17
            12 File(s)     4141056 bytes free
```

The *volume* name BUSINESS is one chosen by the user of this computer and the directory listing indicates that we are looking at Drive C: in the root directory. A root directory is rather like the front cover of a book. Other files can be found in sub-directories.

From the listing you can see there are twelve file names of which some are labelled < DIR >. These DIR names indicate that these are the sub-directories where more files will be stored. Managing files into such directories is an orderly way of storing data on a computer.

The remaining files are needed, in this instance, for booting up the system. As you can observe, you will see that each file is given a date followed by a time which indicates when it was created or last updated. Also, the number following the file name indicates the size of the file.

The line:

12 File(s)   4141056 bytes free

reveals that there are still 4,141,056 bytes of free space on the disk.

CHDIR allows you to CHange DIRectory. In the example above, if you enter the command:

CHDIR MSDOS

you will be in the sub-directory called MSDOS from the root directory. Using the command DIR will give you a list of the files in this directory or in any further sub-directories to this sub-directory.

MKDIR is used to MaKe a DIRirectory. When this command is executed, a new directory is created that is a sub-directory to the one from which it was created.

RMDIR will ReMove a DIRectory. The directory that is to be removed must be empty of any files.

Copying, deleting and renaming files

COPY is used to copy files from source to destination. For example:

COPY   BOOK.TXT A:BOOK.DOC

will copy the file BOOK.TXT from the current disk and directory and produce a copy of it on Drive A with the name BOOK.DOC.

The use of a wildcard symbol (*) allows you to copy a whole series of commands in one go. For example:

COPY *.EXE C:

will copy *all* files with the extension .EXE on them from the current source on to Drive C.

DEL will DELete files. Here, too, the wildcard symbol can be useful. For example:

    DEL *.BAK

will delete all files with the extension .BAK.

REN will REName a file from one to another. For example:

    REN BOOK.TXT BOOK.LST

will alter the directory name of BOOK.TXT to that of BOOK.LST.

Setting paths

PATH = ? is used to tell the computer where to find its software. For example, if we executed the command:

    PATH = C:\MSDOS;C:\

then the operating system would look in the sub-directory MSDOS on C Drive for its program. If it could not be found there, it would look to the root directory on C Drive.

Such paths are normally set from boot-up by inserting the commands in a file called AUTOEXEC.BAT placed in the root directory. This is a file of such MSDOS commands which will be executed on booting up.

Preparing disks

FORMAT is used to format disks. If you acquire new disks, you will need to format them using this command. You can always re-format existing disks, but will erase everything on these disks. For example, entering the command:

    FORMAT A:

will format a disk inserted into Drive A. Formatting sets out the magnetic layout of the disk, allowing the computer both to read data from the disk and to write to the disk in future.

Appendix 5: Details that might appear on a tender document

This appendix is designed to give you a detailed checklist of the information which should influence your choice of supplier, equipment and software as well as information that could be used to get the best out of vendors.

It is useful to have background information on all aspects of the computer system you propose to install. It is not suggested that the first-time buyer should waste time and resources making a full in-depth investigation like that outlined below, but simply keep the basic ideas in mind when shopping around. If, however, you are about to commit your firm to expenditures in excess of, say, £50,000 then you need to gather as much information as possible, on a formal basis, before you make your final decisions.

System supplier

Obtain information regarding the company offering to provide the system, e.g.

- How long it has been trading in its present form and whether it has parent or subsidiary companies.
- Size and scope of the activities of the company, specifying the location of its offices, the number of staff, and especially the number of technical staff.
- Specify any dealerships or other contractual agreements with suppliers of equipment.
- The number of similar systems that the company has installed in organisations similar to your own.
- What support is offered and how it is provided.
- What additional services the company can offer.

Hardware supplier

Obtain information regarding the company offering to provide the hardware, e.g.

- Length of time in business in its present form, and size and scope of activities.
- Its relationship with parent or subsidiary companies.
- Location of offices and factories.
- The number of employees.
- How long the hardware to be supplied has been on the market.
- Whether the manufacturer provides an upgrade path within its range of hardware.
- The number of units of the hardware under consideration that the company has sold.
- Details of the engineering support facilities, number and distribution of engineering support staff, availability of spare parts.

Individual items of hardware

Details should be presented of each item of hardware proposed. An outline of the type of information required is listed below.

For all hardware, the following details should be included:

1. Manufacturer.
2. Physical dimensions.
3. Weight.
4. Electrical details.
5. Power consumption.
6. Heat production.
7. Operating temperature range.
8. Acceptable humidity limits.
9. Noise output.

For the main servers or central processing units:

1. Processor type.
2. Processor speed.
3. Memory requirements.
4. Non-volatile storage details.
5. Access times.

For the terminals:

1. Whether dumb or intelligent.
2. Screen dimensions.
3. Number of lines.
4. Characters per line.
5. Colour or monochrome.
6. Phosphor colour if monochrome.
7. Number and types of interfaces.
8. Details of keyboard.
9. Length of keyboard cable.
10. Compatibility with other equipment.
11. Interfaces available for alien equipment.

For the printers:

1. Type (laser, ink-jet, daisy wheel, etc.).
2. Details of paper feed.
3. Types and weight of paper it can handle.
4. Limitations with thermograph or embossed paper.
5. Number of bins for sheet feed.
6. Number of parts of stationery it can handle.
7. Speed of printing.
8. Number of character sets included.
9. Number of fonts available.
10. Facilities for emboldening, italic, underlining, etc.
11. Whether it supports proportional spacing.

For file storage equipment:

1. Total capacity.
2. Capacity of individual elements.
3. Access times.
4. Method of error checking.
5. Speed of copy.
6. Unit of copy (file, file type, directory, volume).
7. Back-up media.
8. Time required for back-up.
9. Facility for disk mirroring, etc.

Sundry hardware:

1. Modem type and compatibility.
2. Computerised facsimile equipment.
3. Scanner details.
4. Optical character reader features.

5. **Bar code readers.**
6. **Graphics tablets.**
7. **Digitisers.**

Hardware configuration proposed

The hardware supplier should:

- List the equipment and details of the configuration.
- Explain why the configuration has been chosen.
- Outline the expected performance of the configuration.
- Provide information regarding the estimates of memory size, main storage size, system response times for various activities and the onset of degraded performance and its dependence upon system activity.
- Estimate the failure rate and the impact of the failure of particular items on the performance of the system.
- Identify potential failures that might cause loss of data and the precautions proposed to minimise such losses, with special reference to back-up procedures.
- Present details of external requirements such as dedicated telephone lines and associated equipment, indicating responsibility for maintenance and repair of individual items.
- Discuss means by which the security of the system can be maintained in the light of the possibility of unauthorised external access.

Expansion and enhancement of hardware

The hardware supplier should provide details with reference to proposed system and indicate maximum sizes and other limitations, the effect on performance, redundancy of hardware in place and alternative upgrade routes and possibilities for:

---

1. **Addition of further file servers, processors or processor upgrade.**
2. **Additional peripherals.**
3. **Further storage media or upgrades.**
4. **More powerful system.**
5. **Compatibility.**
6. **Compatibility of operating system.**
7. **Compatibility of applications software.**
8. **Transferability of data files and storage media.**

App 5

9. Compatibility of peripherals.
10. Policy regarding trade value of redundant equipment.
11. Implications regarding support and human resources.
12. Delivery.
13. Environmental requirements.
14. Operating system software.
15. Security.
16. Updates and documentation.
17. Applications software.
18. Show how needs are satisfied by proposed system.
19. Software amendments.
20. Communication interfaces.
21. Systems interfaces.
22. Data conversion.
23. Document interchange.
24. Support.
25. Implementation.
26. User training.
27. Hardware maintenance.
28. Software maintenance.
29. Overall implementation.
30. Specialist staff.
31. Time scales.
32. Contractual terms.

Index

abort, 149
abuse, 97
accessing systems, 105, 133, 149, 173
accessories and consumables, 51, 85–6
accounts packages, 22–4, 111
analyst, 149
applications software, 10, *Chapter 10*, 103, 106, 149
assessing computer needs, 2–3
assessing proposals, 64–5
audit trail, 149

backing store, 13–14, 149
backing up data, 15, 42, 110, 127–8, 149, 166
bar codes, 149
batch processing, 42, 99, 150
bench tests, 17
benefits of computerisation, 4–6, 42, 73, 112
bespoke software, 48, 113
bill of materials, 28, 76
bootstrap, 150
breakdowns, 87
BT Gold, 29
budgeting, 59, 62, 64
buffer, 150
bugs, 41, 150
bus, 150
byte, 150

cabling, 80, 101, 135
calculators, 31
calendars, 31
carriage, 150
cash payment method, 88
CBT, 108
CDOS, 10, 133–4
character, 150
clock speed, 16, 150
coding information, 39–40, 70
comfort, 98–9
communications, 29
compatibility, 10, 126

computer aided design (CAD), 150
computer based training (CBT), 108
computer:
  bureau, 151
  programs, 9–10
  systems, 9–11
conditions of service, 53
consultancy, 1, 11, 35, 66, 69
contracts, 123–7
corruption, 151
costs of computerisation, *Chapter 5*
cursor, 151

daisy wheel printer, 151
damaged disks, 97–8
data conversion, 38–40, 113
data processing concepts, 11
Data Protection Act, 161–3, *Appendix 2*
database, 26–7, 151
DataComms, 29
Datel, 151
depreciation, 48, 55
desk top publishing (DTP), 20–1
desks, 101
diagnostic test/routine, 152
diaries, 31
direct computer costs, 47–52
directories in MSDOS, 167
discipline, 112, 135, 136
dot matrix printers, 13, 155
driver, 152
DTP, 20–1

EFTPOS, 152
electricity supply, 96–7, 100
electronic mail, 152
encryption, 127, 129
environmental costs, 50
error message, 105
evaluating systems, 73
exception reporting, 5, 152
exhibitions, 33
expert system, 152

fibre optics, 152
field, definition, 153

file conversion, 38–40, 70–1, 111
file servers, 134
files and records, 27, 40, 153, 167–8
financing computer acquisition, 88–92
floppy disk/drives, 15–16, 104, 129
format, 105, 153, 169
furniture needs, 54

graphics, 30, 135

hacking, 153
handshaking, 153
hard copy, 13, 154
hard disks/drives, 14, 97, 128, 140
hardware:
  costs, 48
  definitions, 9, 154
hazards, 100
heat, 95
housekeeping, 104, 154
humidity control, 96

icon, 154
identifying areas for computerisation, 2
image processing, 154
implementation of applications, *Chapter 11*
indirect computer costs, 53–6
ink-jet printers, 13, 20
installation:
  costs, 80
  of hardware, 80–3
  of software, 15, 33, 38, 64
insurance, 55, 83
integrated software, 31–2
interactive video training, 108
interface, 154
invoicing, 75
ITECs, 165

job, 154
job costing, 28–9

kilobytes, 15, 154
Kimball tag, 154

laser printers, 13, 20, 154

leasing, 89
licences, 136
line printer, 154
loan of equipment, 92
local area network (LAN), 12, 155
logging in and out, 97, 105, 126, 139, 140, 155

mailing and mailshot, 20
mainframe, 155
mains supply, 96–7, 100
maintenance and repair, 43, 50, 82–4, 105, 123–7, 145, 146
malfunctions, 105
management information system (MIS), 155
manuals, 33, 108
megabyte, 14
megahertz (MHz), 17
memory, 15–16
microprocessor, 156
minicomputer, 156
modems, 29, 156
mouse, 17
MSDOS, 10, 133, *Appendix 4*
multiplexor, 156
multi-user systems, 12, 69, 102, 105, 133–5

network, 12, 102, 105, 118, 130, 133–5, 145
network security, 130
noise, 101
nominal ledger, 23, 76
Novell, 134

obsolescence, 34, 55
OCR, 156
off-line, 156
operating systems, 10, 15, 104, 156, *Appendix 4*
OS/2, 10

parallel running, 157
passwords, 105, 129, 130, 157
paths, 169
payment methods, 87–92
payroll, 25–6
peripherals, 80, 157
phasing in systems, 41
posture, 98
Prestel, 29, 157

printing, 13, 51
procedural techniques, 41–2
protocol, 157
publications, 164
purchase ledger, 23, 76
purchase order systems (POS), 72

quotations from vendors, 57

radiation, 100
random access memory (RAM), 16
read only memory (ROM), 16, 157
real-time processing, 157
reflections, 99
remote job entry (RJE), 157
rental, 91
reporting, 3–4, 157
resolution of screens, 30

safety, 100, 101
sales ledger, 22
sales order processing (SOP), 73–5
sampling software, 32–3
scheduling, 158
school leavers, 103
scrolling, 158
security, 104–6, 130, 173–4
serial numbers, 126, 130
servicing, 123–6
silicon chip, 158
soft copy, 13, 158
software:
    costs, 48
    definitions, 10, 158
    support, 54
specifying needs, 58–9
speed, 17
spell checkers, 19
spooling, 158
spreadsheets, 21–2
staff training, 49, 51, 64, 85, *Chapter 10*, 133, 145, 165
standardising software, 32
stand-alone systems, 11, 133, 158
static electricity, 96
stationery, 51, 72, 74
stock control, 23–4, 69–70, 111

storage capacity, 14, 158
storage devices, 13–14, 51
suppliers, of computing, 63, 105, 136, 140, 142, 171
systems analysis, 158

tape streamers, 15, 71
taxation benefits, 89–90
teleprocessing, 158
telex, 158
temperature control, 95
tender documents, *Appendix 5*
terminals, 12, 134
testing of systems, 41
time sharing, 159
training methods, 107–8
training of staff, 49, 51, 64, 85, *Chapter 10*, 133, 145, 165
turnkey systems, 159
tutorials, 33

UNIX, 134
upgrading, 34, 52, 112–13
utility programs, 159

validation, 159
VDU screens, 98–100, 159
vendor choice, 63
ventilation, 96
verification, 159
vibration effects, 97
volatile memory, 16

warranty, 123, 139
word processing, 19–20, 72, 133, 140, 159

Xenix 10, 160